Snacks Under 250 Calories At Home, At
School or Work, On the Go, At a Convenience
Store, or For Your Sweet Tooth

---

365 SNACKS

For Every Day of the Year

BY:

SARAH KOSZYK, MA, RDN

COPYRIGHT

Most photos taken by Sarah Koszyk and Tomas King from Studio 5 Design. http://www.studio5designsf.com/

DEDICATION

To my dear husband, Tomas, whose support, love, and guidance is wonderfully continuous.

To my Mom and Dad for always helping me along the way. I'm forever grateful for the terrific taste buds you gave me.

TABLE OF CONTENTS

39 CHAPTER 3

39 Snacks at School or Work

40	Cooked Oatmeal with Almond Butter
40	Clementines with Walnuts
40	Cucumbers with Yogurt
40	Nonfat Plain Greek Yogurt Parfait
40	Nonfat Vanilla Greek Yogurt with Pumpkin Seeds and Mango
40	Nonfat Plain Greek Yogurt with Walnuts, Cinnamon, and Agave

41	Strawberries and Pineapple with Low Fat Sour Cream
41	Low Fat Cottage Cheese with Blueberries and Almonds
41	Low Fat Cottage Cheese with Sweet Potatoes and Cinnamon
41	Low Fat Cottage Cheese with Cherry Tomatoes
41	Kellogg's® Special K® Protein Fruit & Nut Protein Trail Mix Bar*
42	Lemon Pepper Cottage Cheese Dip with Fresh Veggies
42	Persimmons and Jack Cheese
42	Banana and Almond Butter
42	Prosciutto Wrapped Honeydew
42	Fresh Figs With Goat Cheese and Pecans
42	Laughing Cow® Creamy Swiss Original Spreadable Cheese, Almonds, and Dried Cranberries
43	House Foods® Go Umami Organic Baked Tofu Bar, Hickory Smoke and Grapes*
43	Deli Meat, Celery and Cheese Roll-Ups
43	Tuna with Apples and Walnuts
43	Tuna with Walnuts, Raisins, and Crackers
43	Tuna Bruschetta

44	Pita Pocket with Curried Chicken Salad and Sliced Grapes
44	Veggie Tortilla Wrap with Edamame Hummus
44	Pinwheels
44	Whole Wheat Pita with Peanut Butter and Sliced Peaches
44	Graham Crackers with Almond Butter and Honey
45	Graham Crackers with Peanut Butter and Nutella®
45	Almond Butter and Banana on Whole Wheat Toast
45	Almond Butter and Raisins on Whole Wheat Toast
45	Cashew butter and Peaches on Whole Wheat Toast
45	Peanut Butter and Jelly Waffle
45	English Muffin with Cottage Cheese and Tomatoes
46	Sandwich Thin with Spinach and Cheese
46	Melba Toast with Fat Free Cream Cheese and Dried Cherries
46	Goat Cheese and Apple Crostini
46	Nabisco Triscuits with Cream Cheese and Tiger Sauce
46	Hardboiled Egg on Toast
47	Hardboiled Egg with Apricots
47	Hardboiled Egg with Green Olives
47	Hardboiled Egg with Pistachios
47	Hardboiled Egg with Guacamole
47	Stackers
48	Canned Sardines on Nabisco Triscuits
48	Canned Salmon on Whole Wheat Crackers
48	Canned Chicken on Ak-Mak Crackers

48	Ak-Mak Crackers with Cottage Cheese and Chives
48	Almond Butter and Jam on Ak-Mak crackers
48	Cashew Butter, Honey, and Sliced Apple on Wasa® Crispbread
49	Rice Cake with Almond Butter and Shredded Coconut
49	Rice Cakes with Cream Cheese and Green Onions
49	Rice Cakes with Avocado Spread
49	Trader Joe's® Veggie & Flaxseed Tortilla Chips and Salsa

55   CHAPTER 4

55   Snacks On the Go

69   CHAPTER 5

69   Snacks At a Convenience Store

83   CHAPTER 6

83   Snacks For Your Sweet Tooth

INTRODUCTION

Snacking has always been a huge part of my life. Ever since I was a little girl, we always had snacks at hand. I remember a time when I was just four years old, and my mom took my brother and me to the park to play. We were lucky that the park was only one block from our house so we walked, holding hands. My mom brought chopped up baked potatoes with a little bit of salt sprinkled on them. When we got hungry, she unwrapped the potato chunks, and we happily devoured them. All we knew were those homemade snacks, and we loved them.

Later on when I was eight, I started to play soccer. Every game would have a different parent bringing the snacks. Our family seemed to always have orange wedges for our halftime and a small bag of chips to eat after the game. Chips were a rarity for us at home, so these times were very exciting, and it was a huge treat to have that snack.

I was lucky to have been raised eating whole foods, and foods made from scratch most of the time. My mom is a big planner, and loves to eat, so she generally brought some type of food with us on our outings. However, there were times when we were stuck and needed something small and quick to eat. The local convenience store was the easiest place to go. Unfortunately, not all the options were optimal or "healthy." Luckily, my mom had a degree in Consumer Food Science and was able to navigate the aisles to choose the best snacks possible. Those quick snacks were most often fruit and nuts.

Fast forward to my current life, I've definitely taken many positive traits from my mom, such as bringing snacks with me most of the time. When I decided to help people with their food habits, I knew that I needed to further my food knowledge. So, I obtained a Masters of Arts degree in Family and Consumer Sciences with an emphasis in Dietetics. In addition, I am fully credentialed as a Registered Dietitian Nutritionist (RDN). Throughout all of this, I continue making my snacks at home for my daily routine. Yet, like all humans, I'm not perfect. Sometimes I just need to run into a convenience store and grab that delicious, nutritious snack.

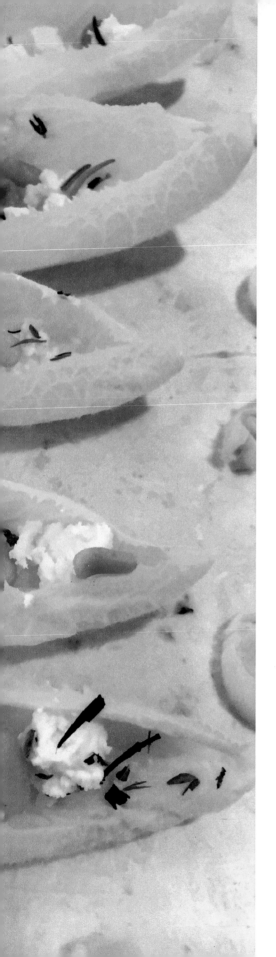

Through my private practice as a dietitian, I see hundreds of families for weight management and healthy living goals. The majority of the families have a hard time determining what snacks are healthy and what snacks are not. There are so many options in the grocery store aisles, and many of these options can be viewed as junk foods. Trying to determine what is "healthy" can be confusing. I wanted to make this book to assist everyone in their mission to eat well and live long.

This book is meant to liberate you through the Power of Snacking! Now you have snack options for every day of the year to enjoy whether you are At Home, At School or Work, On the Go, At a Convenience Store, or just For Your Sweet Tooth. These snacks are each under 250 calories. They are nutritious, healthy, tasty, and dietitian recommended.

Cheers to good eats and fabulous treats!

1 CHAPTER

I'm hungry! Time for a snack

Importance of snacking

Americans are snacking more than ever and trust me, snacking is important. When a person chooses the right snack at the right time, research has suggested that those nutritious snacks can actually help to control weight and improve overall health. Proper snacking can also improve your metabolism, optimize your energy, improve blood sugar control, and better control hunger levels.

Benefits of Snacking

- Increase metabolism
- Optimize energy
- Improve blood sugar control
- Reduce sugar cravings
- Better control hunger levels
- Control weight management
- Improve overall health

This can result in eating less at the main meals and/or choosing healthier food options during the main meals. Other studies suggest that the types of snacks people choose can make a difference in weight management. According to the research, snacks with lots of sugar tend to increase weight versus snacks with more fiber and protein that tend to help people maintain or lose weight.

In addition, snacking can help control our hunger hormone, ghrelin. Ghrelin is the hunger hormone that tells your body you are hungry. Controlling ghrelin can also control blood sugars, increase metabolism, assist with weight management, and reduce sugar cravings. Ghrelin is suppressed while we sleep. When you wake up, it starts to form in the stomach area. Once you eat a meal or snack, you are "full" and ghrelin is suppressed again. Ghrelin will start to produce in the stomach area within 30 minutes of eating your last meal or snack. After three to four hours, ghrelin starts to develop more rapidly and can offset our blood sugars. This can cause people to get shaky, irritable, or light-headed because one's blood sugars have been altered. Eating a snack controls ghrelin, which better controls hunger and increases energy levels. Therefore, eating every three to four hours is very important.

Many people need a snack at least once a day, if not two or three times. The amount of daily snacks depends upon the individual and their activity level and routine. Some of my clients need a morning snack. Some don't. However, ALL of my clients need an afternoon snack between lunch and dinner. Most people tend to crash between 3:00 p.m. and 4:00 p.m.; because they've been working hard all day long and using lots of brain power. When 3:00 p.m. or 4:00 p.m. rolls around, they may start to get sugar cravings or need that afternoon caffeine pick-me-up. This is the time when people debate: "Do I go downstairs to get that cup of coffee where I can also be tempted by the pastry, or do I just stay put and continue to work?" Others might ignore their afternoon hunger and just suffer through it. Unfortunately, when they get home, they will probably devour whatever they can find in the fridge and/or overeat at dinner.

An easy, simple, quick afternoon snack can solve all of these problems: sugar cravings, caffeine cravings, hunger pains, and poor food choices. A healthy snack will nourish you, satisfy you, and control your hunger hormone. My delicious and nutritious snack ideas, will allow you to skip the coffee, soda, or sweets and go for the wholesome, tasty, vitamin-rich snacks to sustain you until dinner or fuel your evening workout.

What is a healthy snack

A healthy snack incorporates both carbohydrates and protein. Ideally, the carbohydrates are also high in fiber. Fiber fills us up to make us feel full.

When you eat a carb/protein snack combination, the protein helps with the uptake of the carbohydrates so you metabolize the carbs more efficiently. Thus, food combining increases one's metabolism.

A simple way to think about this goal is to follow the rule of food combining. Food combination means that you eat at least 2 or more food groups for your snack.

*Food Combination Goal: Always combine at least 2 or more food groups for your snack.

The major food groups are:
Fruits
Vegetables
Grains & Starches
Protein/Meat
Fat
Dairy

Fruit	Vegetables	Grains & Starches
Strawberries	Broccoli	Bread
Blueberries	Cauliflower	Pita
Raspberries	Asparagus	Crackers
Pichuberries	Mushrooms	Corn
Orange	Cucumbers	Peas
Papaya	Spinach	Sweet Potato
Cantaloupe	Tomatoes	Quinoa
Nectarine	Carrots	Rice
Watermelon	Celery	Pasta
Apple	Lettuce	Cereal
Grapes	Eggplant	Granola
Plums	Beets	Legumes

Protein/Meat	Fat	Dairy
Chicken	Nuts	Milk
Fish	Nut Butters	Yogurt
Pork	Seeds	
Beef	Chia Seeds	
Eggs	Ground Flaxseed	
Tofu	Oils (coconut, olive oil, etc.)	
Edamame	Avocado	
Cheese*	Olives	

(*Cheese is classified as a protein since cheese has about 7 grams of protein per 1 ounce serving and 0-1 grams of carbohydrates versus milk that has about 8 grams of protein per 8 ounce serving and 12 grams of carbohydrates).

By combining two or more food groups, you can increase your metabolism and control hunger better.

For example: Have you ever had just a piece of fruit and still felt hungry? Add some peanut butter, almond butter, nuts, cheese, or yogurt to the fruit; and you will feel more satisfied and full. Additionally, you will have more energy to enjoy your day or evening.

How to plan weekly snacks

The idea of snacking can seem overwhelming, daunting, or impossible. I'm here to make your life simpler! Here are some tips about how to plan your weekly snacks:

» Pick 2-3 snacks each week. This way your shopping list is smaller. Everyone will enjoy the same snacks for one week.

» On a Sunday, make 5-10 snack baggies for each person in the family so that everyone has grab-n-go, portion-controlled snacks to eat throughout the week. The number of baggies depends on the person. Some people may need 1 snack per day. Other people may need 2 or more snacks per day.

» The following week or each week thereafter, pick 2-3 new snacks so you don't get bored with what you are eating. Rotating your snacks is also great because it increases variety in your diet.

» If you work, you can bring all the snacks with you on Monday to have your healthy food available throughout the week.

» Set an alarm in your phone or calendar to remind yourself to eat the snack at the designated time each day. If you're in school, you'll eat the snack either between classes or after school.

» Be smart about the timing of your snack. If you know you are starving around 4:00pm (and the *Hangry* comes out), eat the snack at 3:30 p.m. or 3:45 p.m. to better control hunger levels, food cravings, and optimize your mood and concentration. Remember to chew your snack fully to savor the flavors.

» Know Yourself. If you choose to bring a bag of nuts to work for your snack, but you have a hard time controlling how many nuts you eat; don't bring the entire bag. Set yourself up for success by pre-packing the nuts into individual mini-bags. This way, you open one little bag per day and enjoy your portion-controlled, perfect snack.

2 CHAPTER

Snacks At Home

The snacks in this chapter take a little more time and effort to make since you are at home. However, for convenience, you can still pre-prep the snacks or make them in bulk so that they are ready to eat throughout the week during your designated snack time. Here are **80 Snacks at Home**.

Mango Raspberry Smoothie

In a blender, puree all the ingredients for a smooth and fruity treat.

½ cup almond milk + ½ cup frozen raspberries + ½ cup frozen mango + ½ small banana (3 inches, peeled) + 1 teaspoon agave nectar = 160 calories

SarahKoszyk.com

Banana Berry Smoothie

Blend ingredients together for this dessert-like treat. Perfect any time of day.

¼ cup frozen blueberries + ¼ cup frozen strawberries + ½ cup nonfat plain Greek yogurt + ½ cup almond milk + ½ small banana (3 inches, peeled) = 190 calories

Banana Oat Smoothie

In a blender, puree all the ingredients and enjoy.

The added oats make the smoothie thicker so it feels more substantial in your stomach.

¼ cup nonfat plain Greek yogurt + ½ cup nonfat milk + 3 Tablespoons old-fashioned rolled oats + 1 small banana (6 inches, peeled) + 1 teaspoon honey + cinnamon to taste = 240 calories

Pineapple Passion Smoothie

Blend all the ingredients together in a blender for a tropical drink.

½ cup nonfat plain Greek yogurt + ½ cup pineapple juice + ½ small banana (3 inches, peeled) + ½ cup pineapple chunks = 205 calories

Berry-Blaster Smoothie with House Foods® Organic Soft Tofu*

This smoothie has protein from the tofu for a refreshing and filling drink. To make the smoothie, blend all the ingredients together in a blender.

½ cup soft tofu + 1 cup frozen mixed berry medley (blueberries, raspberries, strawberries) + ½ orange, peeled + ½ cup water + 1 teaspoon cinnamon = 180 calories

Kiwi-Berry C-Smoothie

Kiwi and strawberries are chock-full of Vitamin C for you to stay strong and well. Put everything in a blender and blend.

½ cup nonfat + ½ cup nonfat plain Greek yogurt + 1 kiwi (peeled) + ½ cup strawberries = 230 calories

SarahKoszyk.com

Kale Pear Smoothie

This delicious smoothie is sweetened with banana and pear and makes a great vehicle for healthy, fibrous, and iron-rich kale. In a blender, puree all the ingredients.

1 small banana (6 inches, peeled) + 1 cup kale (leaves only) + 1 cup almond milk + 1 small pear, core removed = 205 calories

Classic Green Smoothie

This classic green smoothie is great for a snack. Make it a mini-meal by adding in a scoop of protein powder. The protein will increase the calories and protein grams providing an adequate amount for a small meal. In a blender, puree all the ingredients.

1 small banana (6 inches, peeled) + 1 cup kale (leaves only) + 1 cup spinach
1 green apple, cored + 1 celery stick + juice from ½ a lemon or lime + 1 cup water = 200 calories

Homemade Kale Chips

After you wash the kale, chop the leaves into several pieces. Place on a cookie sheet with a drizzle of olive oil. Bake in a preheated, 375° degree oven for 5 minutes. Flip leaves over and bake for 5 minutes more until kale is crispy and "chip-like." Sprinkle with salt and enjoy.

2 cups kale + 2 teaspoons olive oil = 140 calories

Homemade Zucchini Chips

Slice the zucchini into rounds that are each 1/4 inch thick. Cover a cookie sheet with tinfoil for easy clean-up. Spray the cookie sheet with an olive oil spray. Place the zucchini rounds on the cookie sheet. Spray the zucchini rounds with more olive oil spray. Sprinkle salt on top. Bake at 225° degrees in the oven for 1 hour until crispy. Sprinkle Parmesan cheese on top and enjoy.

1 entire zucchini (2 cups) + ¼ cup shredded Parmesan cheese = 105 calories

Corn On The Cob

Substitute the standard butter-rolled corn on the cob with Greek yogurt to get some protein, too. Cook the corn by boiling it in water for about 5 minutes. Remove the corn from the water. Spread the Greek yogurt on the corn. Sprinkle Parmesan cheese on top. You can also sprinkle chili powder and lime juice on the corn, if you so choose. This is a delicious variation for fresh, corn on the cob.

½ corn on the cob + 2 Tablespoons nonfat plain Greek yogurt + 2 Tablespoons grated Parmesan cheese = 165 calories

Cauliflower Casserole

In a large bowl, mix chopped cauliflower, salt, pepper, and nonfat milk.

Place in a casserole dish and top with 2 Tablespoons breadcrumbs and 2 Tablespoons shredded Parmesan. Bake at 425° degrees for about 30 minutes, until bubbling and cauliflower is fork tender.

Substitute another cheese for the Parmesan cheese such as Gruyere, Asiago, Romano, or Manchego

1 cup cauliflower + 2 Tablespoons breadcrumbs + 2 Tablespoons shredded Parmesan cheese + ¼ cup milk + salt and pepper to taste = 130 calories

Cheesy Roasted Asparagus

Toss asparagus spears with a drizzle of olive oil, salt, and pepper, and grated Parmesan cheese. Roast in a preheated, 400° degree oven until asparagus is tender, about 15 minutes.

8 asparagus spears + 1 teaspoon olive oil + 2 Tablespoons grated Parmesan cheese = 125 calories

Cheesy Roasted Tomatoes

Slice plum tomatoes. Place on a cookie sheet. Sprinkle with breadcrumbs and shredded Parmesan cheese. Broil under high heat until cheese is golden and melted, about 5-7 minutes.

2 plum tomatoes + 2 Tablespoons breadcrumbs + 1 ounce shredded Parmesan cheese = 120 calories

Steamed Artichoke with Tzatziki Dip

Wash the artichoke. Use a sharp knife to cut off the thorns at the top of the leaves. Boil water in a medium sauce pan and add the artichoke to the boiling water. Cover and steam for 45 minutes (make sure the water doesn't all steam out). Remove and drain the artichoke. Dip the leaves into a pre-made tzatziki dip.

1 artichoke + 4 Tablespoons tzatziki dip = 165 calories

Sautéed Broccoli with Pine Nuts and Lemon Zest

For a bright, light side dish or snack, sauté 1 cup trimmed broccoli in 1 teaspoon olive oil in a medium sized sauté pan. Sprinkle with salt and pepper to taste. Remove from heat. Top with lemon zest and ½ ounce of pine nuts.

1 cup broccoli + 1 teaspoon olive oil + ½ ounce pine nuts + salt, pepper, and lemon zest to taste = 185 calories

Roasted Beets with Feta Cheese and Pistachios

Sweet beets, tangy feta and crunchy pistachios are a match made in heaven. Just roast the washed and trimmed beets whole in a baking pan at 425° degrees until they're fork-tender (about 45 minutes). Peel, slice, and season with salt and pepper. Combine with cheese and nuts and enjoy.

½ cup roasted beets + 1 ounce crumbled feta cheese + 15 shelled pistachios = 155 calories

Many grocery stores now sell pre-roasted beets. Use these and either eat them cold or warmed up in the microwave before tossing with the cheese and pistachios.

Cucumber Bites with Cream Cheese and Olives

Spread a little bit of the cream cheese over each sliced cucumber and add half of a pitted black olive to each round. Each round is a fantastic 2-bite snack.

½ cucumber, peeled and sliced in rounds + 2 Tablespoons nonfat cream cheese + 8 pitted black olives, sliced in half = 90 calories

Cucumber Bites with Laughing Cow® Spreadable Cheese and Cherry Tomatoes

Cherry tomatoes and cucumbers are a great combo when stuck together with a cheese spread. Peel the cucumbers. Slice into rounds. Spread some cheese on top and add half a cherry tomato.

½ cucumber, peeled and sliced in rounds + 2 wedges of Laughing Cow® spreadable cheese light (any flavor) + ½ cup cherry tomatoes, sliced in half = 90 calories

Ranch Chicken Lettuce Wrap

Make a quick lettuce wrap by grabbing leftover rotisserie chicken and drizzling ranch dressing on it. Place half of the shredded chicken inside each romaine lettuce leaf. Drizzle each filled leaf with ½ of the dressing to make your own lettuce wraps.

2 ounces shredded rotisserie chicken + ½ Tablespoon ranch dressing + 2 romaine lettuce leaves (makes 2 wraps) = a total of 105 calories for both wraps

Tuscan Kale Wrap

Use kale to wrap up your snack. Make it Tuscan style by using roasted red peppers from a jar with sliced black olives and crumbled feta cheese.

4 slices roasted red peppers + 4 olives, sliced + ½ ounce crumbled feta cheese + 2 kale leaves (makes 2 wraps) = a total of 120 calories for both wraps

Roasted Carrots and Quinoa

Tender carrots pair with quinoa, the protein-packed Peruvian "supergrain." Quinoa is packed with protein and provides additional benefits than other grains. Cook the quinoa according to the package directions. Roast whole carrots on a baking sheet at 400° degrees until tender (about 30 minutes). Place on top of cooked quinoa. Drizzle with a balsamic glaze for a little sweetness.

½ cup cooked carrots + ½ cup cooked quinoa + 2 teaspoons balsamic glaze = 155 calories

Stuffed Bell Pepper

Cut off the top of a bell pepper. Remove the seeds and inside ribs. Stuff with ½ cup cooked barley mixed with chopped basil. Top with feta cheese. Roast at 375° degrees in a small casserole dish for 20 minutes, until cheese is melted and pepper is tender.

1 bell pepper + ½ cup cooked barley mixed with chopped basil (to taste) + 1 ounce feta cheese = 210 calories

Steamed Veggies with Marinara and Parmesan Cheese

You can use fresh or frozen veggies for this. If using frozen veggies, simply steam 1 cup of veggies according to the package directions. If you are using fresh vegetables, then you can prepare them the way you prefer – either steamed in the microwave or in a steamer basket in a saucepan on your cooktop.

I like using a frozen medley package that has cauliflower, broccoli, and carrots that are already pre-chopped. Warm up ½ a cup of marinara sauce from a jar. Mix the veggies with the marinara sauce and sprinkle parmesan cheese over it.

This is a fantastic snack to load up on your vegetables.

1 cup steamed veggies + ½ cup marinara + ¼ cup fresh shredded Parmesan cheese = 170 calories

Edamame and Rice with Reduced-Sodium Soy Sauce

Japanese soybeans and brown rice provide a satisfying snack that's rich in fiber and protein. You can buy fresh edamame already shelled or frozen edamame in a shell. If frozen, simply warm up in the microwave or on the stovetop and remove the beans from the shells.

1 cup shelled edamame + ½ cup cooked brown rice + reduced-sodium soy sauce drizzle = 250 calories

Buckwheat Soba Noodles with Veggies

Soba noodles can be eaten as a snack. Just throw some frozen vegetables and soba noodles into a pot of boiling water. Cook. Drain. Add in reduced-sodium soy sauce for flavor and you've got a fiber and vitamin-filled snack.

½ cup cooked 100% buckwheat soba noodles + 1 cup vegetable mix + 1 teaspoon reduced-sodium soy sauce = 130 calories

Quinoa and House Foods® Organic Firm Tofu*

You can have a quick snack with quinoa and tofu salad. Mix all the ingredients together and you are good to go. Make a bigger batch for leftovers.

House Foods® tofu is very versatile to prepare. You can roast it, eat it raw, marinate it in soy sauce, sauté it, or fry it. There are so many different ways to cook tofu. Try one of these ways for the snack.
*Sponsored Product

½ cup cooked quinoa + ½ cup tofu, chopped + ¼ green bell pepper, diced + ¼ red bell pepper, diced + ½ tomato, diced + 1 Tablespoon fresh basil, chopped + 1 Tablespoon balsamic vinegar + salt and pepper to taste = 180 calories

Homemade Spring Rolls

Make your own fresh spring rolls. Simply get some rice paper and put in water to soften it up. After the rice paper is soft, fill it with lettuce, shredded carrots, julienned cucumbers, fresh cilantro, and sliced tofu. Click HERE for the recipe on how to roll it (or visit SarahKoszyk.com). Enjoy with a sweet chili dipping sauce.

2 rice papers + 1 leaf of lettuce, shredded + 4 slices cucumbers + 1 Tablespoon fresh cilantro + 2 Tablespoons shredded carrots + 4 slices tofu (makes 2 spring rolls) = a total of 220 calories for both rolls

Crunchy Garbanzo Beans with Parmesan Cheese

This snack is great to satisfy a salty-crunchy craving and it's packed with protein. Sprinkle rinsed and drained, canned garbanzo beans with salt and pepper. Bake garbanzo beans for 40 minutes at 400° degrees on a tinfoil-lined cookie sheet (for easy clean up). Remove from oven. Put into a bowl. Toss with the Parmesan cheese. Delicious. Click HERE to watch the video (or visit SarahKoszyk YouTube channel)

½ cup garbanzo beans + 1 Tablespoon shredded Parmesan cheese = 110 calories

Homemade Pita Chips with Tzatziki

Make your own pita chips. Preheat the oven to 400° degrees bake. Rip up half of one whole wheat pita into large chunks. Sprinkle with a little salt. Bake in the oven for 12 minutes and you've got pita chips. Click HERE to watch the video (or visit SarahKoszyk YouTube channel). Dip them into a store-bought tzatziki dip.

½ whole wheat pita bread + salt to taste + 2 Tablespoons tzatziki dip = 130 calories

When looking for a pre-made tzatziki dip, look for brands that use Greek yogurt only. You'll get a lot of protein from this dip.

Homemade Tortilla Chips with Salsa (either prepared or homemade salsa)

Tortilla chips are easy to make. Preheat the oven to 350° degrees bake. Slice up a corn tortilla in any shape you want to have your chips. I like using a pizza cutter to make 6 triangle-shaped chips from 1 tortilla. Sprinkle salt over the tortilla. Bake in the oven on a cookie sheet for 7 minutes and you've got your chips. Enjoy with salsa. This is a really low fat alternative to regular chips and it's homemade.

1 corn tortilla + salt to taste + ½ cup salsa = 105 calories

Homemade Bean Dip with Chips

Drain and rinse a can of black beans. Mix ¼ cup of black beans with ¼ teaspoon garlic powder, ½ Tablespoon lemon juice, and ¼ teaspoon cumin. Puree with a hand-held blender or in a food processor. Make the homemade tortilla chips as previously described to dip into your homemade bean dip.

¼ cup black bean dip (recipe in description above) + 1 corn tortilla (made into chips as described in previously listed snack) = 130 calories

Creamy Beet Dip with Kellogg's® Special K®
Sea Salt Quinoa Crackers*

Beet dip is another version of hummus and is gaining popularity nationwide. You can find beet dip in most grocery stores. Pair this dip with some quinoa crackers for extra protein and fiber.

14 crackers + 2 Tablespoons beet dip = 180 calories

With 130 calories per serving, Kellogg's® Special K® Sea Salt Quinoa Crackers provide a delicious amount of 16 grams of whole grains from wheat, quinoa, oats, and millet, which are naturally low in sugar.

*Sponsored Product

Homemade Nachos

Use the recipe above to make your own tortilla chips using 1 corn tortilla. Shred 1 ounce of cheddar cheese and sprinkle over the chips. Broil in the oven on the same cookie sheet for 3-5 minutes until the cheese is melted. Remove and pour some salsa on the melted, cheesy chips.

1 corn tortilla + 1 ounce shredded cheddar cheese + ½ cup salsa = 205 calories

Edamame Hummus with Red Peppers

Make your own edamame hummus. In a food processor, combine 1 cup cooked edamame, 3 Tablespoons lemon juice, 1 garlic clove, ¼ cup chopped cilantro, 1 Tablespoon olive oil, and salt to taste. Blend. Use red peppers to dip into the edamame hummus. You'll have leftover hummus for another snack.

3 Tablespoons edamame hummus (recipe in description above) + 1 cup sliced red peppers = 95 calories

Fiesta Salad

Combine all the ingredients below to make this delicious salad.

¼ cup canned black beans, drained and rinsed + ¼ cup canned corn, drained and rinsed + ½ cup sliced cherry tomatoes + 1 Tablespoon chopped cilantro + ½ chopped shallot + salt and pepper to taste + 1 Tablespoon white wine vinegar + ½ teaspoon cumin = 230 calories

When buying canned legumes, corn, or green beans, buy reduced-sodium or no salt added products. In addition, drain and rinse the products to remove even more sodium from the reduced-sodium food.

Chicken, Strawberries, and Feta Cheese on Arugula

Here's a great salad to enjoy at home throughout the year. Toss all the ingredients in a bowl and eat.

2 ounces cooked, chopped chicken breast + ½ cup sliced strawberries + 1 cup arugula + 1 ounce crumbled feta cheese = 170 calories

Spinach with Dried Cherries, Pumpkin Seeds, and Crumbled Feta

This flavor combination is so satisfying, and offers a good balance of protein, calcium, and fiber.

3 cups fresh baby spinach + 2 Tablespoons dried cherries + 1 ounce crumbled feta cheese + 1 Tablespoon pumpkin seeds = 200 calories

Caprese Salad

Fresh and summery sliced tomatoes meet calcium-rich cheese for this classic Italian salad. Slice the tomato. Place on a plate and top with thinly sliced mozzarella cheese. Sprinkle chopped, fresh basil leaves on top. Drizzle balsamic vinegar over it. Sprinkle with coarse sea salt for even more flavor.

1 ripe tomato, sliced + 1½ ounces of mozzarella cheese, sliced + 1-2 Basil Leaves, chopped + balsamic vinegar and coarse sea salt to taste = 130 calories

Greek Cheese Plate: Sun Dried Tomatoes, Olives, and Goat Cheese

Here's a healthy Mediterranean-themed snack that's full of flavor. Chop all the ingredients coarsely. Mix and eat.

½ cup sun dried tomatoes + 10 large green olives + 1 ounce goat cheese = 205 calories

Shrimp with Cocktail Sauce

Yes, you can eat shrimp as a snack, too. It's not just an appetizer at a party. Delicious, fresh, and very easy to prepare.

3 ounces of cooked shrimp + 4 Tablespoons cocktail sauce = 140 calories

Poached Egg Over Arugula Salad with Balsamic Dressing

This fresh and easy salad is a great protein source and has choline, which is great for brain health. Mix the spinach with the dressing in a bowl and top with the egg.

1 poached egg + 1 cup raw arugula + 1 Tablespoon light balsamic vinaigrette = 100 calories

Quick Spinach and Mushroom Frittata

Whisk 2 eggs in a bowl with some salt and pepper. Spray an oven-friendly pan with olive oil spray. Sauté the mushrooms over medium heat for 3 minutes. Add fresh spinach. Wilt for about 1 minute. Season with salt and pepper. Add the eggs to the pan and place in an oven that is pre-heated to 325° degrees. Cook for about 10 minutes until the eggs have set.

2 eggs + ¾ cup fresh spinach + ¾ cup fresh mushrooms, sliced + salt and pepper to taste = 230 calories

Avocado, Tomato, and Egg White Omelet

Season whisked egg whites with salt and pepper. Cook over medium-low heat in a nonstick pan until bottom begins to turn golden. Add tomato and avocado. Fold omelet in half and flip. Remove from heat once the eggs are cooked.

1 Tablespoon avocado, sliced + 3 egg whites + 1 small tomato, diced + salt and pepper to taste = 125 calories

Egg White Scramble with Peppers and Goat Cheese

Protein abounds here. Tangy goat cheese and fresh bell peppers add tons of flavor and texture. Spray a small sauté pan with cooking spray. Cook sliced bell peppers over medium-high heat until tender (about 3 minutes). Then whisk 3 egg whites and add to the pan. Top with goat cheese crumbles. Season with salt and pepper. Scramble the mixture until the eggs are cooked.

3 egg whites + ½ cup sliced bell peppers + 1 ounce crumbled goat cheese + salt and pepper to taste = 160 calories

Scrambled Eggs over Wilted Spinach

Whisk 2 eggs. Season with salt and pepper and scramble over medium-low heat in a small, nonstick sauté pan until cooked. Remove from heat. Add the spinach to the pan and let it wilt.

2 scrambled eggs + 1 cup fresh spinach + salt and pepper to taste = 150 calories

Sunny Side Up Eggs and Turkey Bacon

Turkey bacon adds flavor and cuts the fat in this delicious morning snack. Add hot sauce for a bit of spice.

2 sunny side up cooked eggs + 2 slices turkey bacon, cooked = 180 calories

Scrambled Egg over Cooked Brown Rice

Perfect protein and fiber combo snack. Scramble the egg. Flavor with salt and pepper. Top over previously cooked brown rice mixed with rice vinegar for flavor.

1 scrambled egg + ½ cup cooked brown rice + 1 teaspoon rice vinegar = 175 calories

Egg, Spinach, and Cheese Pita Pocket

Scramble the egg whites over medium heat in a small, nonstick sauté pan. Add salt and pepper to taste. After the egg whites cook, add the spinach so it wilts slightly. Stuff the egg and spinach mixture into ½ a whole wheat pita. Add the shredded cheese and tomato slice and you're ready to eat.

½ whole wheat pita + ¼ cup scramble egg whites + ¼ cup chopped spinach + 1 Tablespoon shredded cheddar cheese + 1 tomato slice = 185 calories

Egg Whites and Cheddar Cheese on an English Muffin

Here's a protein power snack augmented by sharp cheddar cheese. Scramble egg whites in a small, nonstick sauté pan over medium-low heat until cooked. Place on a toasted English muffin with sharp cheddar cheese.

2 egg whites + 1 ounce sharp cheddar cheese + 1 whole wheat English muffin, toasted = 225 calories

Easy Egg Salad Wrap with Cucumbers and Carrots

Make the egg salad by using 1 chopped, hardboiled egg mixed with Greek yogurt, celery seeds, and salt and pepper to taste. Put the egg salad onto a whole wheat tortilla. Add 2 Tablespoons shredded carrots and 4 slices of cucumber. Roll up the tortilla to make a wrap and you've got a great snack.

1 egg + ½ Tablespoon nonfat plain Greek yogurt + ¼ teaspoon celery seeds + 2 Tablespoons shredded carrots + 4 slices cucumbers + 1 whole wheat tortilla + salt and pepper to taste = 160 calories

Quick Egg Salad on Half an English Muffin

Just hard-boil an egg, chop it and mix with 1 teaspoon mayonnaise and ½ teaspoon mustard for a protein-rich snack. Serve on a toasted English muffin half.

1 egg + 1 teaspoon mayonnaise + ½ teaspoon mustard + ½ English muffin, toasted = 185 calories

Half English Muffin Tuna Melt

Mix ¼ cup canned tuna with 1 teaspoon low fat mayonnaise and a squeeze of lemon juice. Spread this mixture on the toasted English muffin half. Top with cheese. Broil to melt.

½ 100% whole wheat English muffin, toasted + ¼ cup tuna + 1 teaspoon mayonnaise + ½ Tablespoon lemon juice + 1 slice Jarlsberg® Lite cheese = 235 calories

Whole Wheat English Muffin with Cream Cheese, Smoked Salmon, and Tomato

A fabulous protein-rich snack with a healthy dose of omega-3's from the salmon.

1 whole wheat English muffin, toasted + 1½ Tablespoons low fat cream cheese + 1 ounce smoked salmon + thinly sliced red onion + 1 tomato slice = 250 calories

Toasted English Muffin with Cream Cheese, Tomato, and Cucumber

English muffins are not just for breakfast anymore . Fresh and juicy tomato and cucumber make this perfect for any time of day.

1 English muffin, toasted + 2 Tablespoons low fat cream cheese + ½ cup sliced cucumber + ½ tomato, sliced = 185 calories

Toast with Avocado

Substitute regular butter with avocado by spreading avocado on your toast. Sprinkle a little bit of coarse sea salt on top for a delicious snack. This is wonderfully satisfying, especially if you use a bread with whole grains and seeds. Yum.

1 slice toast + 2 Tablespoons avocado = 125 calories

Toast with Avocado and Melted Cheddar

A classic melted cheese sandwich with added flavor, fiber, and protein. Just spread the mashed avocado on the toast. Top with cheese. Broil for 1-2 minutes in the oven until the cheese melts.

1 slice whole wheat toast + 1 slice cheddar cheese + 2 Tablespoons avocado = 195 calories

White Bean Crostini

Use a whole wheat baguette and slice it into rounds. Toast. Make the white bean mixture by mixing the drained and rinsed canned white beans with ½ teaspoon dried thyme, ¼ teaspoon garlic powder, ½ teaspoon lemon juice, and salt and pepper to taste. Top the baguette slices with the white bean mixture and you've got a nice crostini. You'll also have extra white bean spread for another snack.

4 slices baguette bread, toasted (2 ounces) + 4 Tablespoons white bean spread (recipe in description above) = 180 calories

Quesadilla with Roasted Red Peppers and Mozzarella

Sprinkle mozzarella on a small corn tortilla. Top with roasted red peppers and the second tortilla. Heat in a microwave or cook on the stovetop in a griddle or pan – just long enough to melt the cheese.

2 small corn tortillas (5 inches) + 1 ounce shredded mozzarella cheese + ¼ cup jarred roasted red peppers = 235 calories

Cheese Quesadilla with Avocado and Tomatoes

Melt cheese between two tortillas, then spread mashed avocado on top and cover with halved cherry tomatoes. You can eat it "New York pizza style" by folding it into a half round and then eating it.

2 small corn tortillas (5 inches) + 1 slice or 1 ounce cheddar cheese + ½ cup cherry tomatoes, halved + 1 Tablespoon mashed avocado = 250 calories

Apple and Cheese Quesadilla

Simply slice ½ an apple into thin slices. Put the slices on a corn tortilla with a slice of cheddar cheese. Melt on the stovetop in a pan or griddle or in the microwave.

1 small corn tortilla (5 inches) + 1 slice cheddar cheese + ½ sliced apple = 210 calories

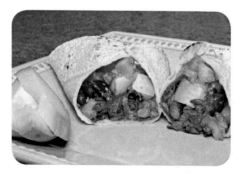

Bean and Guacamole Rollup

Fill one small corn tortilla with ¼ cup mashed black beans and roll it up. Top with 2 Tablespoons avocado and 2 Tablespoons of salsa.

1 small corn tortilla (5 inches) + ¼ cup black beans + 2 Tablespoons avocado + 2 Tablespoons salsa = 180 calories

Tortilla with Pesto and Mozzarella

Herby pesto compliments creamy mozzarella on this low-carb tortilla.

1 high fiber, low carb La Tortilla Factory™ tortilla + 1 Tablespoon basil pesto +2 ounces shredded mozzarella cheese = 185 calories

Turkey and Hummus Wrap

Use a high fiber, low carb tortilla from La Tortilla Factory™ as the wrap. Spread some hummus on it. Top with lettuce, tomato, cucumber, and turkey. Roll the tortilla up for a quick and easy wrap. This is a filling snack.

1 high fiber, low carb La Tortilla Factory™ tortilla + 1 romaine lettuce leaf + 1 slice tomato + 3 slices cucumber + 2 Tablespoons hummus + 2 ounces turkey deli meat = 140 calories

Chicken Kabob with Peanut Sauce

Simply use some leftover rotisserie chicken or roasted chicken breast and put it on a skewer. Dip it into a pre-made peanut sauce for a quick protein snack. Ever noticed that food on a stick always tastes better?

2 ounces roasted chicken breast + 1 Tablespoon peanut sauce = 100 calories

Baked Sweet Potato Fries with Ancho Chili Yogurt Dip

Cut sweet potato into long strips. Toss lightly with olive oil, salt, and pepper. Line a baking pan with tin foil. Spray the tin foil with an olive oil spray. Bake the fries at 400° degrees for about 30 minutes until cooked. While the potatoes are cooking, mix ancho chili powder with nonfat plain Greek yogurt for a flavorful dip for your yummy baked sweet potato fries.

1 cup or 6 ounces sweet potato strips + 1 teaspoon olive oil + ¼ cup nonfat Greek yogurt + pinch of ancho chili powder + salt and pepper to taste = 225 calories

Baked Sweet Potato with a Dollop of Sour Cream

Roast a small sweet potato that has been pricked with a fork and wrapped in tin foil at 400° degrees for 40 minutes. Slice in half, season with salt and pepper, and top with fat free sour cream for an easy and filling snack.

Potatoes have so many different varieties. Try a Russet potato, purple Peruvian potato, red potato, yellow potato, sweet potato, yam, and more.

1 small baked sweet potato (about 6 ounces) + 1 Tablespoon fat free sour cream + salt and pepper to taste = 175 calories

Stuffed Baked Potato

Potatoes are fantastic snacks. You can make them ahead and just add any topping you'd like. Prick the skin of a potato with a fork (to let air and steam release while the potato is cooking). Wrap the potato in tin foil. Bake for 50-60 minutes at 400° degrees. Remove from the oven. Add some salsa for a delicious snack.

1 small baked potato (about 6 ounces) + ½ cup salsa = 185 calories

Baked Potato with Cottage Cheese

Top your baked potato with protein-packed cottage cheese. You get the creamy mouthfeel without the high fat. See the previous snack and learn how to cook a baked potato.

1 small baked potato (about 6 ounces) + ½ cup nonfat cottage cheese = 230 calories

Pizza Crackers

Make a pizza out of Nabisco Triscuit crackers. Spread a little marinara sauce on each cracker. Sprinkle with shredded mozzarella cheese. Top with your favorite veggie (I like using chopped green bell pepper). Broil in the oven until cheese is melted (about 2-3 minutes).

8 Nabisco Triscuit crackers + 3 Tablespoons marinara sauce + 3 Tablespoons reduced-fat mozzarella cheese + ¼ cup chopped veggie of choice = 210 calories

sarahkoszyk.com

English Muffin Pizza

This can be a mini-meal or a hearty snack. Spread ½ a Tablespoon of the tomato paste on each English muffin half. Top each half with a slice of cheese. Toast in the oven until cheese is melted.

1 English muffin + 1 Tablespoon tomato paste + 2 slices Jarlsberg® Lite cheese = 240 calories

Kashi® Waffle 7 Grain with Butter and Blueberry Jam

Just toast a frozen waffle and spread with butter and jam for an easy and delicious snack.

1 Kashi® waffle 7 grain + 1 teaspoon butter + 1 Tablespoon blueberry jam = 185 calories

Black Bean Soup with Sour Cream and Cheddar

There are many options for low fat and low calorie black bean soups. You can also find these soups in boxes. Heat the soup according to the directions on the package. Top with reduced fat sour cream and shredded cheddar cheese for a fantastic mini-meal. My favorite way to eat this snack is in a large mug, sitting on my comfy couch, and savoring the flavors.

1 cup black bean soup + 2 Tablespoons reduced fat sour cream + ½ ounce shredded cheddar cheese = 200 calories

Minestrone Soup and Shredded Cheddar

This comfort food is filling and nutritious. Look for low sodium soup options. Just heat the soup and sprinkle with shredded cheddar cheese.

1 cup minestrone soup + ½ Tablespoon shredded cheddar cheese = 110 calories

Miso Soup with Sashimi

Enjoy this Asian-inspired soup with some fresh fish. You can buy instant miso soup from the store and warm it up when ready to eat. Get fresh, sashimi-grade fish from the market and slice it thin.

1 cup instant miso soup + 2 ounces tuna sashimi (about 2 slices) + soy sauce and wasabi for dipping the sashimi = 105 calories

Half Grilled Cheese Sandwich and Tomato Soup

This "lunch special" is the "diner classic" minus the butter and most of the fat. Use a George Foreman® Grill or a Panini Maker to make this "grilled" cheese with no butter added. Simply put the cheese between the 2 halves of bread and grill it. Serve alongside (or dip into) tomato soup.

SarahKoszyk.com

1 slice whole wheat bread + slice Jarlsberg® Lite cheese + 1 cup tomato soup = 185 calories

Half Grilled Cheese and Apple Sandwich

Adding in the apple gives a crunchy twist on this classic warm sandwich. My favorite apple to use is a Granny Smith green apple. Simply slice it into thin slices and place on top of ½ slice of whole wheat bread. Add 1 ounce slice of cheddar cheese. Top with the other ½ of bread and grill in a George Foreman® Grill or Panini Maker.

1 slice whole wheat bread + 1 ounce cheddar cheese + ½ Granny Smith apple, sliced = 210 calories

Half Turkey Pastrami Panini

Cut 1 slice of whole wheat bread in half. Spread on 1 teaspoon of Dijon mustard on one half of the bread. Add 1 Tablespoon of sauerkraut and an ounce of turkey pastrami. Place the other half of the bread on top. Using a George Foreman Grill® or Panini Maker, heat the sandwich up and you've got a warm Panini sandwich.

1 slice whole wheat bread + 1 ounce turkey pastrami + 1 Tablespoon sauerkraut + 1 teaspoon Dijon mustard = 140 calories

Veggie Cheeseburger

Top a cooked veggie burger with Jarlsberg® Lite cheese for a healthy open-faced veggie cheeseburger.

1 Boca® Burger + 1 slice Jarlsberg® Lite cheese + 1 slice whole wheat bread = 240 calories

Boca® Burger Lettuce Wrap

Warm up a Boca® burger and eat it in a lettuce "sandwich" for some protein-veggie love.

1 Boca® Burger + 2 slices romaine lettuce leaves = 130 calories

3
CHAPTER

Snacks at School or Work

The best way to incorporate snacks for school or work into your routine is to prep them the night or weekend before you need them. My best tip is to pick 2-3 different snacks per week. This way your shopping list is smaller. Then, on Sunday, spend about 10 minutes prepping the snack bags so you just grab-n-go during the week. The following week, rotate your snack options so that you don't get bored. Plus, you will gain the terrific benefit of increased variety in your diet. Enjoy these **80 Snacks at School or Work.**

Barbara's® Puffins® and 1% Milk

This cereal contains wholesome ingredients and comes in great flavors such as Cinnamon and Peanut Butter. Take a carton of milk with you so you have the perfect portion.

¾ cup cereal + ½ cup 1% milk = 170 calories

Bran Flakes with Raisins and 1% Milk

This is a great fiber-rich and filling snack and the raisins add a delicious amount of sweetness.

¾ cup bran flakes + 1 Tablespoon raisins + 1 cup 1% milk = 225 calories

Oatmeal with Fresh Blueberries

This take-anywhere snack is great any time of day. All you will need when you are out is hot water, a bowl, and a spoon. There is usually a microwave to heat it up. If not, you can make it in the morning before you leave and put it in a container.

1 packet dry instant oatmeal + ¾ cup fresh blueberries = 220 calories

Cooked Oatmeal with Almond Butter

The almond butter makes the oatmeal rich, creamy, and hearty while also providing a little protein kick. Make the oatmeal ahead of time. Add the almond butter. Bring to school or work in a mason jar to eat as a midday snack.

1 packet dry instant oatmeal, cooked + ½ Tablespoon almond butter = 210 calories

Clementines with Walnuts

Feeling under the weather and down? Clementines are loaded with Vitamin C to increase immunity and walnuts are a good source of omega-3's to boost your brain power.

2 clementines + 8 walnut halves = 150 calories

Omega-3 fatty acids are heart-healthy fats suggested to improve heart, brain, and skin health. Omega-3s can be found in foods such as sardines, mackerel, tuna, walnuts, flaxseeds, chia seeds, and hemp seeds.

Cucumbers with Yogurt

Slice up cucumbers and dip into plain, nonfat yogurt. You can add flavor to the yogurt by sprinkling cumin powder and salt.

1 cup cucumber, sliced + 1 cup nonfat plain yogurt = 110 calories

SarahKoszyk.com

Nonfat Plain Greek Yogurt Parfait

Layer nonfat plain Greek yogurt with low fat granola, honey, and strawberries for a creamy, crunchy, and sweet snack that packs a powerful protein punch. Put everything in a mason jar and you have an easy to travel snack.

¾ cup nonfat plain Greek yogurt + ¼ cup low fat granola + 1 teaspoon honey + ½ cup sliced strawberries = 165 calories

Nonfat Vanilla Greek Yogurt with Pumpkin Seeds and Mango

A delightful flavor combo with a tropical twist. Put the mango and seeds in separate bags so the seeds keep their crunch. Mix them with the yogurt when ready to eat.

5.3 ounce container nonfat vanilla Greek yogurt + 1 Tablespoon pumpkin seeds + ½ cup mango, peeled and sliced = 240 calories

Nonfat Plain Greek Yogurt with Walnuts, Cinnamon, and Agave

Thick and creamy yogurt is a lovely canvas for aromatic cinnamon, agave, and crunchy walnuts. Put everything in a mason jar and bring to school or work.

5.3 ounce container nonfat plain Greek yogurt + 1 Tablespoon agave nectar + 4 walnut halves, chopped = 175 calories

Strawberries and Pineapple with Low Fat Sour Cream

Mix low fat sour cream with lime juice and cinnamon and use as a dip for strawberries and pineapple slices. Pack it in a mason jar and you're ready for a delicious snack.

4 strawberries + ½ cup pineapple wedges + 2 Tablespoons low fat sour cream mixed with 2 teaspoons lime juice and cinnamon to taste = 115 calories

Low Fat Cottage Cheese with Blueberries and Almonds

Here's a protein and calcium rich combo with antioxidants from the berries.

½ cup low fat cottage cheese + ¾ cup blueberries + 6 almonds chopped = 175 calories

Low Fat Cottage Cheese with Sweet Potatoes and Cinnamon

Get your protein from the cottage cheese and antioxidants from the sweet potatoes for a perfect combo nosh.

½ cup low fat cottage cheese + ½ cup roasted sweet potatoes (see Roasted Sweet Potatoes with Kale snack on page 52, to learn how to roast a sweet potato) + cinnamon for taste = 150 calories

SarahKoszyk.com

Low Fat Cottage Cheese with Cherry Tomatoes

Add some lemon and pepper seasoning to the cottage cheese and tomatoes and you've got a protein-lycopene-rich antioxidant snack.

½ cup low fat cottage cheese + 1 cup cherry tomatoes + lemon and pepper seasoning to taste = 95 calories

Kellogg's® Special K® Protein Fruit & Nut Protein Trail Mix Bar*

This bar is a complete snack in one - providing protein, fiber, and nutrients.

1 bar = 160 calories

Kellogg's® Special K® Protein Fruit & Nut Protein Trail Mix Bars are made from nuts and fruit with a little bit of chocolate love. Plus, these bars provide 8 grams of protein and 4 grams of fiber to fuel you right.
*Sponsored Product

Lemon Pepper Cottage Cheese Dip with Fresh Veggies

Stir pepper and grated lemon zest into ½ cup low fat cottage cheese. Use as a dip for fresh carrots and snap peas.

½ cup cottage cheese + ½ cup carrots + 15 sugar snap peas + lemon zest and pepper to taste = 120 calories

Persimmons and Jack Cheese

Persimmons are delicious snacks. Paired with some cheese, and you have a gourmet indulgence.

1 persimmon (peeled and sliced) + 1 ounce or 1 slice jack cheese = 130 calories

Banana and Almond Butter

A classic combo rich in protein and potassium.

1 medium banana (7 inches, peeled) + 1 Tablespoon almond butter = 200 calories

Prosciutto Wrapped Honeydew

A classic flavor pairing, this can be a surprisingly light snack and a good source of protein.

1 ounce prosciutto + 1 cup honeydew (rind removed, seeded, and cubed) = 115 calories

Fresh Figs With Goat Cheese and Pecans

Halve fresh figs and spread with goat cheese, then top with pecans.

2 medium figs + ½ ounce spreadable goat cheese + 4 pecan halves = 155 calories

Laughing Cow® Creamy Swiss Original Spreadable Cheese, Almonds, and Dried Cranberries

This healthy cheese plate is creamy, sweet, and nutty.

2 wedges of Laughing Cow® creamy Swiss original spreadable cheese + 6 almonds + 2 Tablespoons dried cranberries = 205 calories

House Foods® Go Umami Organic Baked Tofu Bar, Hickory Smoke and Grapes*

These ready to eat tofu bars are packed with 5 grams of protein. Pair with some grapes for a well-balanced snack.

1 House Foods® Go Umami Baked Tofu Bar + 17 grapes = 120 calories

House Foods® Go Umami Baked Tofu Bars are vegan, have no preservatives and they're the first ever tofu snack that's individually packaged for protein on the go. They're non-GMO and gluten free, too. Try other flavors like Savory and Orange Teriyaki.
*Sponsored Product

Deli Meat, Celery and Cheese Roll-Ups

Just roll sandwich meat and sliced cheese around a celery stalk for a quick snack with a satisfying crunch.

1 stalk of celery + 1 slice or 1 ounce lean deli meat + 1 slice provolone cheese = 135 calories

Tuna with Apples and Walnuts

Mix the tuna with Greek yogurt, diced apples and chopped walnuts. Add garlic powder, dill, salt, and pepper to taste. You've just made a tuna salad. Put it in a container and you can eat it at school or work.

3 ounces canned tuna, drained + ½ apple, diced + 4 walnuts, chopped + 2 Tablespoons nonfat plain Greek yogurt + garlic powder, dried dill, salt, and pepper to taste = 195 calories

Tuna with Walnuts, Raisins, and Crackers

Put the walnuts, raisins, and crackers in a separate bag. Bring the tuna in a small container or mini-can or bag (the stores now sell tuna in a bag). Mix these all together when you are ready to eat your snack. I like using Ak-Mak crackers since they have a good source of fiber.

3 ounces tuna, drained + 4 walnut halves + 1 Tablespoon raisins + 4 Ak-Mak crackers = 245 calories

SarahKoszyk.com

Tuna Bruschetta

This Mediterranean snack will transport you to the beaches of southern Italy... almost! Chop tuna and cherry tomatoes. Season with salt, pepper, and chopped basil. Place on a slice of toasted whole wheat bread. This can easily be packed ahead and taken to school or work.

2 ounces canned tuna, drained + 1 cup cherry tomatoes + 1 slice whole wheat toast = 175 calories

Pita Pocket with Curried Chicken Salad and Sliced Grapes

Make this quick chicken salad ahead of time to bring to school or work: ¼ cup of cooked and chopped, skinless chicken breast mixed with 1 teaspoon light mayonnaise and a pinch of curry powder. Fill a half pita pocket with the chicken salad and halved grapes for the perfect sweet and savory combo.

½ whole wheat pita pocket + ¼ cup chicken salad (recipe in snack description) + 8 grapes = 230 calories

Veggie Tortilla Wrap with Edamame Hummus

Using edamame hummus is a great switch from regular hummus and adds extra protein to this veggie delight wrap. Use a high fiber, low carb flour tortilla from La Tortilla Factory™.

One high fiber, low carb flour tortilla from La Tortilla Factory™ (10 inches) + 2 Tablespoons edamame hummus + 2 slices tomato + 1 romaine lettuce leaf + 3 slices cucumber + ¼ cup sprouts = 115 calories

Pinwheels

Grab a flour tortilla and spread it with nonfat cream cheese. Place a layer of deli ham on top of the cream cheese. Sprinkle some chopped scallions on it. Roll up the tortilla to make a burrito and you've got your pinwheel. Wrap it up and bring it to school or work.

One high fiber, low carb flour tortilla from La Tortilla Factory™ (10 inches) + 2 Tablespoons nonfat cream cheese + 2 slices or 2 ounces 98% lean deli ham + chopped scallions to sprinkle = 140 calories

Whole Wheat Pita with Peanut Butter and Sliced Peaches

Fresh fruit replaces jelly in this twist on a classic PB & J.

½ whole wheat pita + 1 Tablespoon peanut butter + 1 peach, sliced = 240 calories

Graham Crackers with Almond Butter and Honey

Almond butter is a great substitute for peanut butter for people with allergies. The honey adds extra sweet love to this creamy, delightful snack.

3 graham crackers + 1 Tablespoon almond butter + 1 Tablespoon honey = 240 calories

SarahKoszyk.com

Graham Crackers with Peanut Butter and Nutella®

Peanut butter and this chocolaty hazelnut spread provide a perfect combination with the graham cracker crunch. Use 2 graham crackers to make a sandwich with the peanut butter & Nutella® as the fillings inside.

2 graham crackers + ½ Tablespoon of peanut butter + ½ Tablespoon of Nutella® = 200 calories

Almond Butter and Banana on Whole Wheat Toast

Here's a different version of Elvis' favorite snack.

1 Tablespoon almond butter + ½ small banana (3 inches, peeled and sliced) + 1 slice whole wheat toast = 210 calories

When buying bread, look at the nutrition label for the Dietary Fiber. It will usually list the grams of fiber per slice of bread. Buy products with at least 3 grams of fiber. 5 grams or more is ideal.

Almond Butter and Raisins on Whole Wheat Toast

Just spread the love on the bread and you'll be a happy camper.

½ Tablespoon almond butter + 2 Tablespoons raisins + 1 slice whole wheat toast = 225 calories

Cashew butter and Peaches on Whole Wheat Toast

Modify the previous recipe by using a different nut butter and a different fruit. The options are open. I used peaches because they are delicious.

1 Tablespoon almond butter + ½ peach, sliced + 1 slice whole wheat toast = 210 calories

Peanut Butter and Jelly Waffle

Instead of using bread to make a sandwich, take a frozen waffle from your freezer. Toast it and spread it with peanut butter and jelly. It's a nice twist to the classic snack.

1 Kashi® waffle 7 grain, toasted + ½ Tablespoon peanut butter + ½ Tablespoon jelly = 160 calories

English Muffin with Cottage Cheese and Tomatoes

A whole wheat English muffin topped with creamy cottage cheese and sweet and juicy tomatoes makes for a satisfying combo. Plus, you get a nice dose of protein to boot.

1 whole wheat English muffin, toasted + ¼ cup cottage cheese + 8 cherry tomatoes =180 calories

Sandwich Thin with Spinach and Cheese

Using Laughing Cow® cheese, spread it onto a sandwich thin. Top with some spinach for iron and Vitamin K.

1 sandwich thin + 1 wedge of Laughing Cow® spreadable cheese light + ¼ cup fresh spinach leaves = 125 calories

Melba Toast with Fat Free Cream Cheese and Dried Cherries

Spread cream cheese on melba toast and top with sweet dried cherries. Yum!

4 slices melba toast + 2 oz. fat free cream cheese + 2 Tablespoons dried cherries = 180 calories

Goat Cheese and Apple Crostini

I like using Musso's™ Oven Baked Crostini crackers. Spread some goat cheese on the crackers and put a sliced apple on top. Delicious snack.

4 Musso's™ oven baked crostini crackers + 1 ounce goat cheese + 1 small apple = 240 calories

Nabisco Triscuits with Cream Cheese and Tiger Sauce

This simple snack is completely revamped by drizzling Tiger Sauce over the cream cheese. You can find Tiger Sauce in most grocery stores. It's a sweet sauce with a little spice. Put the cream cheese and Tiger Sauce in a small container with a snap on lid. The crackers go into a sealable plastic baggie to keep them crispy. Easy breezy.

8 Nabisco Triscuits + 2 Tablespoons nonfat cream cheese + 2 teaspoons Tiger Sauce = 180 calories

Hardboiled Egg on Toast

This is a protein and fiber rich power snack. Just slice the hardboiled egg when you are ready to eat and place on top of the mustard smeared toast. The mustard adds tons of flavor and makes the snack special.

1 hardboiled egg + 1 slice whole wheat toast + 1 Tablespoon Dijon mustard = 150 calories

Hardboiled Egg with Apricots

A simple protein and carbohydrate combination. It's fun to eat a bite of egg and then a bite of apricot.

1 hardboiled egg + 5 dried apricots = 130 calories

Hardboiled Egg with Green Olives

This power snack packs protein, heart-healthy fat, and flavor.

1 hardboiled egg + 10 large green olives = 115 calories

Hardboiled Egg with Pistachios

Bring on the protein power. Eat side by side.

1 egg hardboiled + 15 pistachios = 115 calories

Hardboiled Egg with Guacamole

Protein abounds in this filling and sustaining snack.

1 hardboiled egg + 2 Tablespoons guacamole = 115 calories

Stackers

Stackers have basic ingredients: crackers, cheese, deli meats, pickles, cucumbers, and sliced apples. You can stack up the layers any way you want. Mix and match the flavors.

2 Ak-Mak crackers® + 1 slice Jarlsberg® Lite cheese, cut into 4 pieces + 1 ounce turkey deli meat, cut into 4 pieces + 4 pickle rounds or cucumber slices + 4 slices apple = 200 calories

Canned Sardines on Nabisco Triscuits

Sardines are a wonderful source of omega-3's which are fabulous for heart, brain, and skin health. Prep the sardines by mashing them slightly and mixing with mustard. Put it in a small container with a lid and you're off. The crackers go in a separate bag.

2 ounces canned sardines, drained + 1 teaspoon mustard + 6 Nabisco Triscuits = 225 calories

Canned Salmon on Whole Wheat Crackers

Get your omega-3's from canned salmon. Spread it on some crackers. If you have a lemon handy, drizzle on some juice, too.

3 ounces canned salmon + 5 whole wheat crackers with no fat added + lemon juice (optional) = 240 calories

Canned Chicken on Ak-Mak Crackers

Make your chicken salad before going to school or work by mixing 2 Tablespoons nonfat plain Greek yogurt, a sprinkle of dried dill, and lemon and pepper seasoning with the canned chicken. Serve over crackers.

3 ounces chicken salad mixture + 4 Ak-Mak crackers = 170 calories

Ak-Mak Crackers with Cottage Cheese and Chives

Fiber and flavor come together with these crackers topped with protein-rich cottage cheese and flavorful herbs.

5 Ak-Mak sesame crackers + ½ cup nonfat cottage cheese + chives to garnish = 150 calories

Almond Butter and Jam on Ak-Mak crackers

Classic PB & J is revamped with a modified twist for extra fiber from the crackers.

4 Ak-Mak sesame crackers + 1 Tablespoon almond butter + 1 Tablespoon raspberry jam = 225 calories

Cashew Butter, Honey, and Sliced Apple on Wasa® Crispbread

Spread sweet and nutty cashew butter on 2 Wasa® crispbreads. Drizzle with honey and top with apple slices for a sustaining snack.

1 Tablespoon cashew butter + 2 Wasa® crispbreads + 2 teaspoons honey + ½ small apple sliced = 250 calories

Rice Cake with Almond Butter and Shredded Coconut

Almond butter and coconut is a perfect combo on this crunchy rice cake.

1 rice cake + 1 Tablespoon almond butter + 1 Tablespoon sweetened, shredded coconut = 165 calories

Rice Cakes with Cream Cheese and Green Onions

Spread cream cheese on 2 rice cakes and sprinkle with fresh and bright green onions for a zippy flavor.

2 rice cakes + 2 Tablespoons cream cheese + ½ cup chopped green onions = 190 calories

Rice Cakes with Avocado Spread

Cut up an avocado and spread it on each rice cake. This snack is delightfully crunchy, and you get heart-healthy fat from the avocado. Sprinkle with a little salt and/or your favorite spice or herb for flavor.

2 rice cakes + 2 Tablespoons avocado = 125 calories

Trader Joe's® Veggie & Flaxseed Tortilla Chips and Salsa

These flaxseed chips offer fiber, omega-3's, and antioxidants without sacrificing flavor. Pair with fresh salsa for a great snack.

15 Trader Joe's® veggie & flaxseed tortilla chips + ½ cup salsa = 150 calories

Black Beans with Salsa Salad

Drain a can of black beans and rinse to remove any excess sodium. Mix the black beans with salsa and add 2 Tablespoons of nonfat, plain Greek yogurt for a creamy bean salad. NOTE: You'll have leftover beans from the can to use in another meal or snack.

½ cup black beans + ½ cup salsa + 2 Tablespoons nonfat, plain Greek yogurt = 145 calories

Pretzel Crisps® and Guacamole

These thin pretzel chips are a new way to enjoy a classic combination of chips and guacamole. You can find ready-made guacamole at most stores.

1 ounce Pretzel Crisps® + 4 Tablespoons guacamole = 195 calories

Baked Pita Chips and Guacamole

These baked chips are a great, healthy alternative to potato chips, without sacrificing that savory crunch. (You can also make your own pita chips by toasting a pita in the oven with some salt for 12 minutes at 400° degrees, bake. Click HERE for the recipe or visit SarahKoszyk page on YouTube.com.

11 pita chips + 2 Tablespoons guacamole = 155 calories

Rice Crackers with Roasted Red Pepper Spread

Try using a roasted red pepper spread instead of hummus for a yummy change. Pair with rice crackers.

15 rice crackers + 2 Tablespoons roasted red pepper spread = 160 calories

Rice Crackers and Curried Yogurt

Just add curry powder to plain nonfat Greek yogurt and you have a flavorful dip for these crunchy crackers.

15 rice crackers + ¼ cup nonfat plain Greek yogurt + curry powder = 170 calories

Pita and Baba Ghanoush

This Middle Eastern eggplant dip is smoky and hearty.

1 whole wheat pita pocket + 2 Tablespoons store-bought baba ghanoush (Middle Eastern eggplant spread) = 225 calories

Sugar Snap Peas and Tzatziki

Fresh snap peas add a sweet crunch to creamy store bought tzatziki. You can also make your own tzatziki. Click HERE for the quick and easy recipe or watch the video at SarahKoszyk page on YouTube.com.

15 pea pods + 3 Tablespoons store bought tzatziki cucumber and yogurt dip = 130 calories

Fresh Broccoli and Hummus

Tasty and low fat. This snack will keep you going throughout the day.

1 cup raw broccoli florets +1/3 cup store bought hummus = 145 calories

Make your own hummus. It's very easy. Click HERE for the recipe or watch the video at SarahKoszyk page on YouTube.com.

Red Bell Pepper and Hummus

Get a satisfying crunch with fresh bell pepper dipped in creamy hummus.

1 cup sliced bell peppers + 1/3 cup hummus = 145 calories

Baby Carrots and Edamame Hummus

Edamame hummus has more protein than regular hummus. Pair it with the baby carrots for a protein-packed twist on the classic snack.

2 Tablespoons edamame hummus + 1 cup baby carrots = 125 calories

Ranch Dip Crudité

This is a great, fresh snack idea with lots of fiber. You can use any combination of raw veggies here.

2 Tablespoons store-bought ranch dip + ½ cup raw broccoli + ½ cup raw carrots + ½ cup raw celery = 165 calories

Make a healthier version of the ranch dip using nonfat plain Greek yogurt. Get the recipe HERE or watch the video at SarahKoszyk page on YouTube.com.

Sliced Cucumber with Sheep's Milk Cheese

Sheep's milk cheese such as feta or Spanish manchego has a characteristic tang and a satisfying saltiness, which pairs deliciously with mild, fresh cucumber.

1½ cups sliced cucumber + 1 ounce sheep's milk cheese = 95 calories

Ham and Jicama

Simply wrap the ham slice around the jicama strip and you've got a protein snack with a crunch.

1cup jicama (peeled and sliced into strips) + 2 ounces 98% lean deli ham = 95 calories

Romaine Leaves with Laughing Cow® Garlic and Herb Spreadable Cheese and Chopped Walnuts

Simply spread the cheese onto the romaine leaves and top with chopped walnuts for a fun finger food.

2 wedges of Laughing Cow® garlic and herb spreadable cheese + 4 romaine leaves + 4 walnut halves, chopped = 110 calories

Endives with Goat Cheese and Pine Nuts

Use an herbed goat cheese and spread it onto the endive leaves. Sprinkle pine nuts on top for some extra crunch.

8 endive lettuce leaves + 1 ounce herbed goat cheese + 2 Tablespoons pine nuts = 170 calories

Endives with Ricotta

Add some low fat ricotta cheese to an endive leaf and you've got a savory, quick snack. Make ahead and bring to school or work. You can also top with your favorite dried herb or seasoning for another flavor.

8 endive leaves + ¼ cup low fat ricotta cheese = 60 calories

Roasted Sweet Potatoes with Kale

Toss 1 cup sweet potato slices with 1 teaspoon olive oil, salt, and pepper. Roast at 400° degrees for 25 minutes. Serve with 1 cup of kale that you have sautéed in a pan sprayed with olive oil spray. This is easily made ahead and can be eaten at room-temperature at school or work. Enjoy your vegetable power snack.

1 cup sweet potatoes, sliced + 1 teaspoon olive oil + 1 cup chopped kale + olive oil spray + salt and pepper to taste = 230 calories

Roasted Sweet Potatoes with Parmesan Cheese

Roast a small sweet potato that has been pricked with a fork and wrapped in tin foil at 400° degrees for 40 minutes. After it cooks, add parmesan cheese. You can prep the snack on the weekend for an easy grab-n-go snack during the week.

½ cup sweet potato + 2 Tablespoons grated parmesan cheese = 135 calories

Cobb Salad

A simplified version of a classic salad that is filled with protein. Mix all of the ingredients together. Put in a sealable container and you're good to go.

1 ounce chopped turkey breast (no skin) + 1 chopped hardboiled egg + 3 cups raw spinach + 2 Tablespoons light ranch dressing = 205 calories

Spinach and Tangerine Salad

Adding a citrus component to a salad brings a burst of freshness and flavor. Mix the spinach with tangerine wedges, balsamic vinegar, olive oil, salt, and pepper to taste. Put the salad in a mason jar for easy travel.

2 cups spinach + 1 tangerine + 1 teaspoon balsamic vinegar + 1 teaspoon olive oil + salt and pepper to taste = 90 calories

2-Bean Salad

Drain canned garbanzos and black beans. Rinse the beans to remove excess salt. Mix with crumbled goat cheese, fresh arugula, a squeeze of lemon juice and a drizzle of olive oil for a hearty, fibrous snack. Bring it to work or school for a pre-prepped snack that's easy to eat at your desk.

1/3 cup canned garbanzo beans + 1/3 cup canned black beans + ½ cup raw arugula + ½ ounce crumbled goat cheese + 1 teaspoon olive oil + squeeze of lemon juice + salt and pepper to taste = 230 calories

Green Bean Medley Salad

Mix all the ingredients in a bowl at home. You can use canned beans. Just drain and rinse them to get rid of any excess sodium.

¼ cup canned green beans + ¼ cup wax beans + ¼ cup garbanzo beans + ½ Tablespoon lemon juice + garlic powder, salt, pepper, oregano, thyme, basil, and lemon and pepper seasoning to taste = 125 calories

Tomato and Roasted Red Pepper Soup with Crumbled Goat Cheese

Just top this sweet and savory Tomato and Roasted Red Pepper Soup with tangy goat cheese crumbles for a great, quick snack.

1 cup soup + ½ ounce goat cheese crumbles = 160 calories

Sushi-time

Grab a 6-piece sushi roll and eat that as a snack. Make sure to buy the small rolls with just 1 or 2 items inside the rice. You can also make your own sushi and take it with you. Click HERE for the recipe or visit SarahKoszyk.com.

6-piece small sushi roll = 155 calories

4
CHAPTER

Snacks On the Go

A snack "On the Go" is a snack you can throw in your purse, briefcase, or backpack and eat after a few hours. Some of these snacks can be bought "as is" from your grocery store. The rest of these snacks can be pre-prepped the night before. Either way, when you are ready to leave, you just grab your snack and run out the door. Ready for a fabulous day. Enjoy **80 Snacks On the Go.**

Apple Rings and String Cheese

Dehydrated apples are a great portable snack and taste delicious alongside a savory string cheese. Look for dried apple rings with no added sugar. The ingredients should just say "apples."

6 dried apple rings + 1 light string cheese = 145 calories

Apple and Cheddar Cheese Wraps

Grab an apple. Slice it. Wrap a slice of cheddar cheese around the apple slices.

1 medium apple + 1 slice cheddar cheese = 190 calories

Apple and Milk

This is a tried and true quick snack. Grab a fruit with a crunch, such as an apple, and pair it with a mini carton of milk for some protein.

1 small apple + 1 cup (8 ounce) nonfat or 1% milk = 150-160 calories

Gouda and Dried Apricots

This filling snack takes almost no preparation and can be eaten on the go.

1 ounce Gouda cheese + 5 dried apricot halves = 140 calories

String Cheese and Apricots

Stone fruit season offers a plethora of delicious and otherwise unavailable fruits such as juicy ripe apricots. Enjoy with protein and calcium rich string cheese. You can substitute apricots with your favorite stone fruit such as 1 peach, 2 plums, or 1 nectarine.

I light string cheese + 2 fresh apricots = 105 calories

Cheddar Cheese and Red Grapes

This super easy snack packs protein, calcium, and just enough fat to satisfy.

1 ounce cheddar cheese + 17 red grapes = 170 calories

Cheddar Cheese and Cherry Tomatoes

Tomatoes and cheese go so well together. Cut cheese into chunks and you're off to go.

1 ounce cheddar cheese + 1 cup cherry tomatoes = 165 calories

Grape Tomatoes and Goat Cheese

Throw the tomatoes and cheese in a bag and you're off to a running start.

1 cup grape tomatoes + 1 ounce goat cheese = 125 calories

Prosciutto and Figs

This Mediterranean inspired snack satisfies the salty-sweet cravings. Wrap the prosciutto around the figs for a deliciously tasty treat.

2 ounces prosciutto + 3 dried figs = 165 calories

Figs and Parmesan Cheese

Parmesan cheese is a lean protein. Pairing this salty cheese with the sweet dried figs is a match made in heaven.

3 dried figs + 1 ounce Parmesan cheese = 175 calories

Watermelon with Feta and Mint

A fresh summertime salad that can be made ahead and packed to go. Feta is another salty cheese that works beautifully with the sweet melon and aromatic mint.

1 ¼ cups watermelon, rind removed and cubed + 1 ounce crumbled feta + chopped mint leaves = 130 calories

Apple and Peanut Butter

Peanut butter goes so well with apples and this snack is perfect for an on-the-goal fuel. Slice the apple in half. Cut out the core. Put the peanut butter in between the 2 apples halves. Wrap it up and take it with you.

1 medium apple + 1 Tablespoon peanut butter = 190 calories

Banana and Cashew Nut Butter

Cashew nut butter is gaining more popularity throughout the United States. Pack the cashew nut butter in a small container along with a small knife or spatula. When you are ready to eat, spread it on a peeled banana for a well-balanced snack.

1 small banana (6 inches, peeled) + 1 Tablespoon cashew nut butter = 190 calories

Dried Mango and Cashews

This tangy tropical dried fruit is a great pairing with the rich taste of crunchy, toasted cashews. Make sure to buy dried mango that doesn't have any added sugar in the ingredients.

¼ cup dried mango + 6 cashews = 200 calories

> Fruit has natural sugar. When buying dried fruit, make sure the ingredients list only the fruit and not "fruit, sugar." This way you know you are just buying the natural dried fruit. Some dried fruits, such as cranberries, will have added sugar in order to be edible.

Dried Apricots and Brazil Nuts

Fibrous apricots and rich, satisfying Brazil nuts are a match made in heaven.
5 dried apricot halves + 6 Brazil nuts = 160 calories

Dried Pichuberries with Sacha Inchi Seeds

Pichuberries and Sacha Inchi seeds are Peruvian powerfoods. Sacha Inchi seeds have an incredible amount of omega-3's. Pichuberries are super high in Vitamin C. And both have protein. Get ready to live long and strong.

15 sacha inchi seeds + 37 pichuberries = 135 calories

Pear and Pecans

Pair a pear with some pecans for a quick snack on the go. Pleasantly perfect.

1 pear + 4 pecans = 165 calories

Pomegranate and Pine Nuts

This fruit takes time to peel which can slow down how fast you eat it. Pair it with some nuts for a well-balanced combination snack. Be sure to pack a few napkins to catch any pomegranate squirts.

1 pomegranate (6 ounces edible part) + ½ ounce pine nuts = 210 calories

Pomegranate and Pistachios

Another super fun combo to eat with the pomegranate fruit: pistachios. Lay out your napkin so you can pick out the pomegranate seeds and open up the pistachio nuts. Enjoy working for this snack.

1 pomegranate (6 ounces edible part) + 15 pistachios = 165 calories

Cherries with Pine Nuts

When in season, cherries are very sweet. The pine nuts offer the savory factor. Pre-prep this snack by washing the cherries, letting them air dry, and then putting them in a small bag with the pine nuts.

1 cup cherries with pits + 1 Tablespoon pine nuts = 175 calories

Date Balls

Pre-make this snack for a quick nibble on the go. Using a food processor, combine dates, walnuts, salt, and cinnamon. Remove the crumbly mixture to a small bowl and add the honey. Mix and roll it up into 4 balls. Now, you've got date balls.

3 dates + 4 walnuts + salt and cinnamon to taste + ½ Tablespoon honey = 210 calories

Roasted Cauliflower with Pine Nuts

Sprinkle the cauliflower with salt and pepper and bake for 20 minutes in a preheated oven at 450° degrees. Drizzle with 2 Tablespoons balsamic vinegar. Let cool. Put in a to-go container with some pine nuts and you've got a great snack on the go. (You can also roast the pine nuts with the cauliflower).

1 cup roasted cauliflower + 2 Tablespoons balsamic vinegar + 1 ounce pine nuts = 215 calories

Nonfat Greek Pumpkin Yogurt

This is a perfect combination snack in one package. Get your protein on and get filled up.

1 container (5.3 ounces) nonfat Greek pumpkin yogurt = 205 calories

Nonfat Plain Greek Yogurt with Banana

Greek yogurt topped with sliced banana is a sweet and creamy snack with a healthy dose of protein and potassium.

1 container (5.3 ounces) nonfat plain Greek yogurt + 1 small banana (6 inches, peeled and sliced) = 205 calories

Cucumbers and Cottage Cheese with Basil

Slice up some cucumbers and add it to cottage cheese. Sprinkle basil on top and you've got a protein-powered snack. Put this in a container with a lid for a snack on the go.

½ cup low fat cottage cheese + 1 ½ cups sliced cucumber + basil = 95 calories

Low Fat Cottage Cheese with Fresh Mango

Protein, calcium, and fruit in one portable power snack.

½ cup low fat cottage cheese + ½ cup fresh mango (peeled and sliced) = 130 calories

Pineapple and Red Pepper Skewers

Slice some red peppers and get some pineapple chunks. Make a kabob by placing the fruit and veggie on a skewer or tooth pick. You have a quick snack on the go.

1 cup red pepper + 1 cup pineapple chunks = 105 calories

Jicama with Fresh Mango

Pre-pack a snack bag with sliced jicama and mango. Squeeze some lime juice on it and you're off on the run for a crunchy sweet snack.

½ cup jicama, peeled and sliced + 1 cup fresh mango, peeled and sliced + lime juice to taste = 130 calories

Jicama with Cucumbers

Another great Latin-flare snack. You can also add lime juice and sprinkle chili powder on it.

2 cups sliced jicama + 1 cup sliced cucumber + lime juice and chili powder to taste = 110 calories

Sugar Snap Peas, Red Grapes, and Laughing Cow® Spreadable Cheese

This delicious combo snack is great for the green and red-colored produce. The cheese gives you a little protein. Try spreading the cheese on the sugar snap peas.

15 sugar snap peas + 17 grapes + 1 wedge of Laughing Cow® spreadable cheese light = 110 calories

Sliced Turkey and Grapes

This super simple snack goes a long way to stave off hunger - thanks to lean protein.

1 ounce sliced turkey + 17 grapes = 95 calories

Turkey and Pickle Wraps

Wrap sliced turkey breast around a crunchy dill pickle for a salty, crunchy snack.

3 ounces turkey deli meat + 3 dill pickle spears = 105 calories

For all these snack ideas containing deli meats, you can substitute any meat you want. For example, try lean roast beef. Look for deli meats that are nitrate and nitrite free.

Turkey Lettuce Wrap

Lay down one large romaine lettuce leaf and spread with mustard. Top with 1 slice of reduced fat provolone and 1 slice deli turkey. Roll like a burrito and enjoy. Wrap it up for a snack on the go. It's delicious.

1 romaine lettuce leaf + 1 teaspoon mustard + 1 slice deli turkey + 1 slice reduced fat provolone = 105 calories

Turkey Roll-Up

Wrap deli turkey meat around a dill pickle spear and a light string cheese for a carb-free "sandwich."

2 ounces sliced deli turkey meat + 1 light string cheese + 1 dill pickle spear = 125 calories

Turkey Breadstick Rollups

Just roll meat and cheese around a crunchy breadstick. This recipe makes 2 rollups.

2 slices turkey breast + 2 slices reduced fat provolone + 2 sesame bread sticks = a total of 215 calories for both rollups

Buffalo Chicken Wraps

Grab a tortilla, wrap it around some roasted chicken breast from last night's dinner or a leftover rotisserie chicken. Spread some barbeque sauce on it. Now you've got a tasty snack on the go.

1 small corn tortilla (5 inches) + 1 ounce chicken breast + ½ Tablespoon barbeque sauce = 130 calories

Beef Jerky and Figs

This salty-sweet combination snack also provides you with the carbs and protein you need to stay energized.

1 ounce beef jerky + 3 dried figs = 145 calories

Individual Tomato Basil Frittata Muffins: To Go

Preheat an oven to 375° degrees bake. Whisk together 6 eggs, 2 ounces crumbled goat cheese, ¼ cup basil pesto, and 1 diced tomato. Season with salt and pepper to taste. Divide mixture into 6 muffin molds in a metal muffin tin that has been sprayed with non-stick spray. Bake until tops are puffed and set, about 14 minutes. Makes 6 individual frittata muffins. Now you can grab-n-go that delicious snack throughout the week.

1 egg frittata muffin = 115 calories

Egg Muffins with Kale and Cheese

Becky Rosenthal from Vintage Mixer posted this amazing recipe for egg muffins using kale, cheddar cheese, and some spices. Click HERE for the recipe (or visit SarahKoszyk. com) and enjoy this simple make-ahead snack. It's perfect when running around town and wanting some hearty protein (from the eggs and cheese) and vitamin C & A (from the kale).

1 egg muffin = 110 calories

Red Pepper, Spinach, and Cheese Frittata

Make a 12-egg frittata on the weekend. Slice it into 12 slices. Wrap up each slice and you've got a snack on the go with veggies and protein. Click HERE for the easy and quick recipe (or visit SarahKoszyk.com)

1 frittata slice = 150 calories

Bagel Thin with Almond Butter and Raisins

Choose any flavor of bagel thin and top with creamy almond butter and sweet and chewy raisins. The bagel thins have the flavor and texture of a bagel but a lot less carbs for a perfectly portioned snack.

1 bagel thin + 1 Tablespoon almond butter + 2 Tablespoons golden raisins = 220 calories

Bagel Thin and Nutella®

This chocolate hazelnut spread is just dreamy on a toasted bagel thin.

1 bagel thin, toasted + 1 Tablespoon Nutella® = 180 calories

Strawberries and Cream Cheese Sandwich

Make a sandwich by slicing 3 fresh strawberries and putting them onto a slice of bread spread with cream cheese. It's a tea party on the go.

1 slice whole wheat bread + 1 Tablespoon nonfat cream cheese + 3 strawberries, sliced = 130 calories

When buying bread, read the nutrition facts label and buy breads with at least 3 grams of dietary fiber or more per slice of bread. 3 grams of fiber/slice is good. 5 grams of fiber/slice is excellent.

Half PB & B Sandwich

Peanut butter and banana sandwiches are delicious and can provide a great snack on the go.

1 slice whole wheat bread + 1 Tablespoon peanut butter + ½ small banana (3 inches, peeled and sliced) = 225 calories

Nabisco Wheat Thins Whole Grain Crackers with Goat Cheese and Grapes

Halved grapes and tangy, spreadable goat cheese make a great topping for whole grain Nabisco wheat thins.

8 Nabisco wheat thins + 1 ounce goat cheese + 17 grapes = 240 calories

Multi Grain Pretzels and String Cheese

Perfect for when you're on the move - pretzels and string cheese will keep you going.

15 multi grain pretzels + 1 piece of light string cheese = 135 calories

Multi Grain Pretzels and Beef Jerky

Carbs and protein combine for this salty, crunchy, chewy snack on the go.

15 multi grain pretzels + 1 ounce beef jerky = 165 calories

Multi Grain Pretzels with Peanut Butter and Fruit

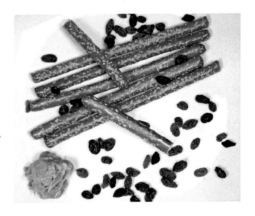

Use the peanut butter as a dip for the pretzels and stick on some dried cranberries or raisins. Now you have a "wand" for your snack.

15 multi grain pretzels + ½ Tablespoon peanut butter + 1 Tablespoon dried cranberries or raisins = 195 calories

Ak-Mak Crackers with Goat Cheese

Grab a few crackers with high fiber and pair it with protein-filled goat cheese.

4 Ak-Mak crackers + 1 ounce goat cheese = 180 calories

Rice Crackers with Wasabi Peas

This Asian-inspired crunch mix is great when running around town and wanting some spice.

15 rice crackers + ¼ cup wasabi peas = 240 calories

Pumpkin Spice Muffin

This 3-ingredient, easy-to-make, quick pumpkin muffin is an amazing snack. Make a batch on the weekend so you can grab-n-go all week long. Click HERE for the recipe (or visit SarahKoszyk.com).

1 pumpkin muffin = 190 calories

Applesauce Banana Muffins

I love applesauce banana bread. It's so easy to make. Instead of using a bread pan, I put the batter in a muffin tin to make. Click HERE for the recipe (or visit SarahKoszyk.com) and you can eat your muffins on the go.

1 applesauce banana muffin = 145 calories

Use this recipe to make a small, mini-loaf to give to people during the holidays as a healthy, delicious present. You can include the recipe with the loaf.

Rhythm Superfoods® Roasted Kale with Sea Salt*

When you're running around town and want a salty, crunchy snack - roasted kale is the answer. A crispy superfood at its finest.

1 package (0.75 ounces) Rhythm Superfoods® Roasted Kale with Sea Salt = 100 calories

Rhythm Superfoods® Roasted Kale is rich in Vitamins A and K. Rhythm Superfoods® offers 5 flavors of Roasted Kale and 7 flavors of its dehydrated kale chips.

*Sponsored Product

Chewy Granola Bar

A chewy granola bar adds fiber and nut protein on the go. Find bars with at least 5 grams of fiber per serving.

I granola bar = 150 calories

Feta Stuffed Olives

Prep this snack at home and pack it for the day. Stuff black pitted olives with a little bit of feta for some Mediterranean bliss.

16 black pitted olives + 1 ounce crumbled feta cheese = 160 calories

Roasted Red Pepper Stuffed Olives

Use roasted red peppers from a jar. Slice them into tiny strips to fit inside black pitted olives. Get some veggies while also getting a heart-healthy fat from the olives.

16 black pitted olives + 1 roasted red pepper, sliced = 105 calories

Black Olives and Baby Carrots

This fun snack can be used to make mini wands by sticking the black pitted olive onto the end of the baby carrot. Or just mix everything into a bag for simplicity.

1 cup baby carrots + 16 pitted, large black olives = 115 calories

Kashi® GO-LEAN Cereal with Blueberries

Combine 1 cup of the cereal with 1 cup of fresh blueberries in a bag and you've got a high-fiber, high-protein, antioxidant super snack.

1 cup Kashi® GO-LEAN cereal + 1 cup blueberries = 220 calories

Kellogg's Nutri-Grain® Bar and Apple

These cereal bars pack whole-grain fiber into a small, portable and convenient package and are delicious paired with a juicy apple.

1 Kellogg's Nutri-Grain® bar + 1 small apple = 180 calories

Kellogg's Strawberry Nutri-Grain® Bar with a Banana

This is a classic combination of pairing strawberries with bananas for an easy on the go snack.

1 Kellogg's Strawberry Nutri-Grain® bar + 1 small banana (6 inches) = 210 calories

Kellogg's Nutri-Grain® bars come in a variety of flavors and most include 3 grams of fiber per serving. Switch up the flavor and switch up the additional fruit choice for more variety.

*Sponsored Product

Cantaloupe and Gingersnaps

Sweet melon and cookies with a snap are a great pairing.

3/4 cup cantaloupe (rind removed, seeded, and cubed) + 3 small gingersnaps = 140 calories

Goldfish Crackers and an Apple

Cheesy goldfish paired with a juicy apple makes an easy snack on the go.

55 goldfish crackers (30 grams) + 1 small apple = 200 calories

Rhythm Superfoods® Beet Chips Naked* with Fruit

Where's the beet? It's right here and it's delicious. There's just one ingredient in this package: beets. That's it. They're loaded with fiber and packed with iron and calcium. Pair them with a fruit for a fabulous combination

1 package (1.4 ounces) Rhythm Superfoods® Beet Chips Naked + 1 fruit of choice = 160 calories

Rhythm Superfoods® is a trusted brand that makes non GMO, gluten free, and vegan snacks that are minimally processed with only a handful of real ingredients.

*Sponsored Product

Popcorn and Raisins

Sweet and salty come together in this take-anywhere snack. Make the bags ahead of time for easy travel.

3 cups air-popped popcorn + 2 Tablespoons raisins = 140 calories

Popcorn and Dry-Roasted Chick Peas

Grocery stores now sell dry-roasted chick peas in individual packages. Pair it with some popcorn for a crunchy-salty snack.

3 cups air-popped popcorn + 10 dry-roasted chick peas = 160 calories

Popchips® and Clementines

These crunchy chips come in lots of great flavors and are a great stand-in for fried potato chips. Pair with juicy clementines.

1 small bag of popchips® (0.8 ounces) + 2 clementines = 155 calories

Wasabi Peas

Wasabi peas are very fun and great for on-the-go adventures. You can clear your sinuses with this snack. A tiny bit truly goes a long way. There's also protein in the peas for a delectable combination.

¼ cup wasabi peas = 130 calories

Seaweed Snack Pack and Edamame

You can now find these individual seaweed snack packs at most stores. Grab it while grabbing some edamame beans and you're out the door with a protein-powered plant-based snack.

1 seaweed snack pack + 1 cup edamame (in the shells) = 155 calories

Edamame and Tangerines

Get your Vitamin C from the tangerines and your protein from the edamame.

2 tangerines + ½ cup shelled-edamame = 130 calories

Broccoli Florets and Light Ranch Dressing

This easy portable snack offers the nostalgic and delicious flavor of ranch dressing with fresh, raw broccoli.

1 cup broccoli florets + 2 Tablespoons light ranch dressing = 100 calories

Cherry Tomatoes and Hummus

Sweet, juicy cherry tomatoes and creamy hummus make for a great anytime/anywhere snack.

1 cup cherry tomatoes + 1/3 cup hummus = 145 calories

Cucumber, Roasted Red Peppers, and Ricotta

Here's a great play on a Greek salad that can easily be pre-prepared and eaten on the go. Put all the ingredients in a tightly sealed container. When you are ready to eat, simply shake it to mix.

1 ½ cups cucumber, chopped + ½ cup roasted red pepper slices, chopped + ¼ cup ricotta, crumbled + 1 teaspoon olive oil + 1 teaspoon red wine vinegar = 180 calories

Carrots and Peanut Butter

Yes: dip the carrots into peanut butter and you've got a satisfying snack with Vitamin A to help your eyesight.

1 cup baby carrots + 1 Tablespoon peanut butter = 125 calories

Ants on a Log, Traditional

Celery, peanut butter, and raisins make this traditional snack delectable.

2 celery stalks + 1 Tablespoon peanut butter + 2 Tablespoons raisins = 165 calories

> For the Ants and Beetles on a Log recipes, make them portable by placing the insides with the filling of both stalks together and wrapping in plastic wrap. This way, there is less mess when you open the snack.

Ants on a Log, Updated

Almond butter replaces peanut butter and dried cherries replace raisins in this updated version of a classic snack.

2 celery stalks + 1 Tablespoon almond butter + 2 Tablespoons dried cherries = 175 calories

Beetles on a Log

Spread hummus onto celery sticks and place halved, pitted kalamata olives on top for a "beetle" on a log.

3 celery sticks + 3 Tablespoons hummus + 8 large olives cut in half = 125 calories

Celery and Laughing Cow® Creamy Swiss Original Spreadable Cheese

Laughing Cow® cheese is so versatile and delicious. Spread it on celery for a quick & easy snack.

4 stalks celery + 2 wedges of Laughing Cow® creamy Swiss original spreadable cheese = 115 calories

Half Baked Potato and Cheese Stick

My mom used to take us to the park when we were kids and bring a cut-up baked potato with salt sprinkled on it. Pair it with a cheese stick for a carb-protein combo snack.

½ baked potato sprinkled with salt + 1 light string cheese = 135 calories

Vegetable Juice and Whole Grain Crackers

Here's a convenient way to get your veggies on the go.

1 cup vegetable juice (such as V8®) + 15 whole grain baked crackers (such as Nabisco Wheat Thins) = 210 calories

Vegetable Juice and Turkey

Get your veggies on with some turkey deli meat on the side for protein.

1 cup vegetable juice (such as V8®) + 2 ounces turkey deli meat = 120 calories

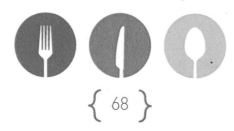

5
CHAPTER

Snacks At a Convenience Store

I'm always an advocate of making your snacks and bringing them with you when you are out and about running errands, traveling, etc. Sometimes you might not have time to plan or prep a snack. Or other times, you may be traveling where there is no option for a pre-planned snack, especially if you have been on the road for many days. At these times, the convenience store could be your only option. Eating a snack is important to maintain energy and control hunger levels. Some of the foods suggested are available in regular size packages, so remember to take out the recommended portion. You'll have extra food for subsequent snacks.

Here are **80 Snacks At a Convenience Store.**

Graham Crackers and Milk

Yes, this tried and true classic snack is meant for everyone. You can buy individual cartons of milk just like when we were in school.

8 ounce carton of nonfat milk + 3 graham crackers = 170 calories

Nabisco Wheat Thins and String Cheese

You can find this great combo snack anywhere. These crackers are a good source of fiber and string cheese offers a healthy serving of protein.

1 single serve bag of Nabisco Wheat Thins or 16 crackers + 1 string cheese = 200 calories

Crackers and Swiss Cheese Slice

Buy the box of crackers and the bag of sliced Swiss cheese to have for a few snacks and not just one.

4 crackers + 1 slice cheese = 185 calories

Crackers and Laughing Cow® Light Spreadable Cheese Wedge

Spread the cheese on the crackers for a tasty snack.

4 crackers + 2 wedges of Laughing Cow® light spreadable cheese = 140 calories

Breadsticks with Laughing Cow® Light Spreadable Cheese Wedge

Use the breadstick to dip into the cheese. Laughing Cow® light cheese wedges are available in multiple flavors. Choose the one that makes you the happiest.

2 breadsticks + 2 wedges of Laughing Cow® light spreadable cheese = 150 calories

Carr's® Whole Wheat Crackers and Cheddar Cheese Stick

Pair these together for some fiber and protein.

4 crackers + 1 cheese stick = 250 calories

Sesame Snack Stick with a Cheese Stick

Sesame snack sticks are fun and made with honey. Pair them with some cheese for a complete snack.

1 ounce sesame snack sticks + 1 cheese stick = 230 calories

Special K® Cracker Chips with Mozzarella String Cheese

Crackers and cheese is a timeless snack perfect on the run.

30 Special K® cracker chips + 1 cheese stick = 180 calories

Mary's Gone Crackers® with Dried Cranberries

These crackers are gluten free and very satisfying when eaten with dried cranberries.

13 Mary's Gone crackers® + 1 Tablespoon dried cranberries = 170 calories

Crackers with Salsa

Want a special twist from the typical chips and salsa? Try crackers.

13 crackers + ½ cup salsa = 155 calories

Pretzels and Cheddar Cheese Stick

Good ol' classic pretzels are a healthy choice and can be found almost anywhere.

1 ounce pretzels + 1 cheese stick = 180 calories

Pretzels with Applesauce

Dip the pretzels in the applesauce for some extra flavor and a totally different tasty treat.

1 ounce pretzels + ½ cup applesauce = 165 calories

Pretzels and Raisins

Mix pretzels with raisins. It's a yummy combo snack.

1 ounce pretzels + 1 box of raisins = 155 calories

Crackers and Hummus Snack Pack

Hummus with crackers is a perfect snack. Many companies now make 2 ounce snack packs to go.

4 crackers + 2 ounce hummus snack pack = 210 calories

Pita Bites with Hummus Snack Pack

Try pita bite chips with the hummus snack pack.

9 pita bites + 2 ounce hummus snack pack = 195 calories

Justin's® Almond Butter Squeeze Pack with Wasa® Crispbreads

Justin's® almond butter squeeze packs are great snacks when you're at a convenience store. Pair them with any whole grain cracker and you're golden with a great combo snack.

1.15 ounce Justin's® almond butter squeeze pack + 1 Wasa® crispbread = 235 calories

Justin's® Almond Butter Squeeze Pack with Rice Cakes

You can add the almond butter to a rice cake for another convenient snack.

1.15 ounce Justin's® almond butter squeeze pack + 2 rice cakes = 250 calories

Justin's® Almond Butter Squeeze Pack with Raisins

Add the almond butter to a fruit for a power-packed snack.

1.15 ounce Justin's® almond butter squeeze pack + ½ ounce box of raisins = 230 calories

Baked Potato Chips with Dried Cranberries

A great sweet and savory on-the-go snack. These baked chips cut fat but still offer great crunch and texture.

1 ounce (15-20) baked chips + 2 Tablespoons dried cranberries = 140 calories

Baked Lentil Chips with Salsa Pack

Chips and salsa time. Baked chips are lighter than regular chips. This modified version of chips using lentils provides a little extra protein.

22 baked lentil chips + ½ cup salsa pack = 135 calories

Toasted Coconut Chips

These chips are naturally made with healthy coconut oils for a hearty snack with iron.

0.7 ounce package toasted coconut chips = 115 calories

Crisp Baked Apple Chips with Cheese

Look for brands that have baked apple chips with no sugar added and no preservatives. Basically, you are just eating dehydrated, baked apples. Pair with some cheddar cheese for extra love.

1 ounce or ½ cup baked apple chips + 1 cheddar cheese stick = 190 calories

Cinnamon Apple Chips with Nuts

There are even flavored apple chips out there.

0.7 ounce package cinnamon apple chips + 12 almonds = 150 calories

Roasted Garbanzo Beans (a.k.a. Chickpeas)

Companies are now roasting garbanzo beans (a.k.a. chickpeas) for a crunchy snack. This is a combo snack because oil is used during the roasting process.

½ cup roasted garbanzo beans = 150 calories

Snap Pea Crisps Any Flavor

Snap Pea Crisps are another version of salted, dehydrated vegetables. There's oil in the crisps for a combination snack.

22 snap pea crisps = 120 calories

Pirate's Booty® Veggie Snacks

These chip-like snacks are a great alternative to the regular chip. And they're made of vegetables, too.

2 ounces Pirate's Booty® veggie snacks = 120 calories

Nice!® Veggie Sticks

Another alternative for dehydrated vegetables in a chip-like form. Crunchy and salty.

1 ounce Nice!® veggie snack = 130 calories

Microwave Popcorn and Sunflower Seeds

Look for small bags of microwave popcorn that are air-popped with no added butter. Add a few sunflower seeds to give you the salty kick.

1 ounce air-popped popcorn bag + 1 Tablespoon salted sunflower seeds = 205 calories

Microwave Popcorn and Dates

What better way to enjoy a date than with some popcorn...and a movie?

1 ounce popcorn bag + 3 dates = 190 calories_

Animal Crackers and Apricots

While you may not have had them since elementary school, these sweet animal crackers are delicious, fun as ever, and make a great, quick snack. Enjoy with some dried apricots on the side.

16 animal crackers + 5 dried apricots = 180 calories

Nabisco Fat Free Fig Newtons Snack Pack

Pre-portioned packs offer controlled snacking for these fat free treats. It is a delicious combo of "fruit and cake."

2.1 ounce Nabisco Fat Free Fig Newton Snack Pack (2 cookies) = 200 calories

SarahKoszyk.com

Granola Bars

Granola bars are very satisfying.

1 bar = 160 calories (amounts may vary depending upon the brand)

Look for granola bars with minimal ingredients and ingredients you can pronounce. Also look at the nutrition label for bars with at least 3 grams of dietary fiber or more. 5 grams or more of dietary fiber is an excellent choice.

Whole Grain Cereal Cups – Cheerios® and Raisins

These are pre-portioned cereal cups and come in healthy favorites, such as Cheerios®. Eat it dry and add some fruit to make your own trail mix.

30 gram, pre-portioned cup of Cheerios® + 2 Tablespoons raisins = 200 calories

Kefir Lowfat Plain with Cheerios®

Kefir is a yogurt-like drink. Many people can tolerate kefir who may not be able to tolerate regular milk. Try kefir with cereal.

1 cup lowfat plain kefir + ½ cup Cheerios® = 180 calories

Hot Cereal Oatmeal Cups

Many companies now offer oatmeal or other hot cereals in a cup where you just need to add hot water. Many have dried fruit already included in the cups. Most convenience stores have microwaves to heat it all up.

2.6 ounce container of hot cereal = 250 calories

KIND® Fruit and Nut Bars like Raspberry Cashew & Chia

These are all natural food bars made with wholesome ingredients. There are many more delicious flavors, so have fun choosing your favorites.

1 KIND® fruit and nut bar = 180-200 calories

Dark Chocolate and Walnuts

Satisfying that chocolate craving does not need to break the calorie bank. Rich, intense dark chocolate is a much smarter choice than a regular candy bar, and packs much more chocolate per calorie. Look for bars with at least 70% cocoa or more for extra antioxidants and richness.

1 ounce dark chocolate + 4 walnut halves = 205 calories

KIND® Snacks are a healthy go-to product choice. They are made with ingredients you understand and can pronounce, such as fruit, nuts, seeds, and/ or whole grains. In addition, they're a combination snack all in one package.

*Sponsored Product

Almonds and String Cheese

Just a simple, easy snack. Eat the almonds slowly to really fill you up and satiate your body.

12 almonds + 1 string cheese = 230 calories

Dried Apricots with Cheese and Almonds

Enjoy 3 different food groups together for a perfect balance of carbohydrates, protein, and fat.

5 dried apricots halves + 1 mini Babybel® Light cheese round (1 ounce) + 6 almonds = 165 calories

Dried Cranberries and Cashews

Enjoy this simple mix.

1 Tablespoon dried cranberries + 12 cashews = 120 calories

Dried Apricots and Pistachios

This snack is easy peasy and can be purchased at most convenience stores.

5 dried apricot halves + 15 pistachios = 105 calories

Prunes and Pecans

Fruit & nuts are a quick snack to keep you going strong. Did you know that prunes are dried plums and a good source of Vitamin A?

3 prunes + 8 pecans = 150 calories

Dates and Peanuts

Dates are extremely sweet. Pair with some salty peanuts for a delectable, sweet and salty combination.

3 dates + 10 peanuts = 135 calories

Dried Mango and Pumpkin Seeds

Add some sweet and spicy to your salty treat for a Latin flare. Try the dried mango with chili powder and salted pumpkin seeds.

¼ cup dried mango + 1 Tablespoon pumpkin seeds = 200 calories

Dried Papaya and Sunflower Seeds

Dried fruit is fantastic. Look for versions with no added sugar. Check the ingredients and make sure it just states the fruit of choice and not "fruit, sugar."

¼ cup dried papaya + 1 Tablespoon sunflower seeds = 200 calories

Applesauce with Pumpkin Seeds

Look for applesauce that has "no sugar added." Applesauce is naturally sweet so you don't need more sugar.

½ cup or 1 small container of applesauce + 2 Tablespoons pumpkin seeds = 140 calories

Pressed by KIND™ Mango Apple Chia*

This is an all-natural, vegan bar. This particular bar is made with only 3 ingredients - just the two fruits and chia seeds.

1 Pressed by KIND™ Mango Apple Chia bar = 130 calories

Pressed by KIND™ bars are made with only fruit & chia or fruit & veggies (and no added sugar). They are a good source of fiber providing 3 grams of fiber per serving.

*Sponsored Product

Cashews and Canned Peaches

Canned peaches may remind you of your childhood, but pre-packaged fruit cups are a great and speedy choice for a healthy snack at any age. Add a few cashews to make a perfect combo snack.

½ cup canned peaches + 6 cashews= 105 calories

Pumpkin Seeds and Fruit Cup

Look for fruit cups in water instead of syrup. The label will state "no sugar added." Pair with some pumpkin seeds or pepitas for a little protein.

1 fruit cup + 2 Tablespoons pumpkin seeds (a.k.a. pepitas) = 130 calories

Mozzarella Cheese and Fresh Fruit Cup

Many convenient stores are now offering fresh fruit cups filled with cantaloupe, pineapple, grapes, and more. Pair it with a nice stick of mozzarella cheese and you have a perfect combination snack.

8 ounce cup of fresh fruit + 1 mozzarella cheese stick = 175 calories

Trail Mix

Perfect for a hike in the wilderness or a day in the urban jungle. Trail mix can keep you nourished while on the move.

¼ cup trail mix = 170 calories

Wasabi Peas and Almonds

Get a spicy kick with the wasabi peas. Adding in some almonds can give you that extra savory heart-healthy fat.

1/3 cup wasabi peas + 6 almonds = 195 calories

Corn Nuts and Raisins

Corn nuts are a great snack on the go. Pair them with raisins for some sweetness and phytonutrient love.

1/3 cup corn nuts + 2 Tablespoons raisins = 170 calories

Pistachios and Raisins

Pistachios are wonderful because they take time to open each nut. So this snack will last longer which adds to your enjoyment.

15 pistachios + 1.5 ounce box of raisins = 175 calories

Peanuts in the Shell and Cheese

This throwback snack is packed with Vitamin E, heart-healthy fats, and protein. Since portion control is key with nuts, shelling your own peanuts slows you down so you don't over-consume.

20 peanuts + 1 mini Babybel® Light cheese round (1 ounce) = 150 calories

Banana Chips and Pecans

Most banana chips are made with oil and salt, so you have to watch the portions of these dehydrated fruit chips. The amount listed here is the perfect portion size.

1/3 cup banana chips + 4 pecans = 195 calories

Banana and String Cheese

Plain and simple. You can find these options almost anywhere. A great go-to when you're out and about.

1 small banana (6 inches, peeled) + 1 string cheese = 160 calories

Banana and Peanuts

What better way to enjoy bananas with nuts than this?

1 small banana (6 inches, peeled) + 10 peanuts = 135 calories

Orange and Sunflower Seeds

Oranges are very easy to find at a convenient store since they hold up so well. Pair it with some sunflower seeds and you have a well-balanced snack.

1 orange + ½ cup sunflower seeds in the shells = 195 calories

Seaweed Snack Pack and Orange

Enjoy a salty seaweed snack with a citrusy orange on the side.

1 seaweed snack pack + 1 orange = 120 calories

Beef Jerky with Dried Cranberries

Beef jerky can be a low fat snack to get your protein. Cranberries add the sweet.

1 ounce beef jerky + 2 Tablespoons dried cranberries = 140 calories

Beef Jerky with a Pear

Try pairing beef jerky with a fresh piece of fruit such as a pear. It's exquisite.

1 ounce beef jerky + 1 pear = 205 calories

Turkey Jerky with Pistachios

Try a turkey jerky for some different flavored, salty protein enjoyment.

1 ounce turkey jerky + 15 pistachios = 145 calories

Salmon Jerky with Macadamia Nuts

Get ready for some tropical bliss by pairing salmon jerky with macadamia nuts.

1 ounce salmon jerky + 5 macadamia nuts = 180 calories

Hardboiled Egg and Apple

Convenience stores now have eggs boiled, peeled, and ready to eat; offering a great, quick-fix option for hunger.

1 hardboiled egg + 1 medium apple = 135 calories

100% Vegetable Juice and Apple

Here's a great, convenient way to get your veggies and fruits while on the go.

1½ cups vegetable juice (such as V8®) + 1 medium apple = 135 calories

Single Serve Packages of Baby Carrots and Hummus

Simple with a satisfying crunch, carrots with hummus are a great choice for a healthy snack on the go.

1 mini-package (2.5 ounces) raw baby carrots + 1 single-serving (2 ounce) container of hummus = 175 calories

Single Serve Packages of Baby Carrots and String Cheese

Cheese really does go well with most foods, especially veggies.

1 mini-package (2.5 ounces) raw baby carrots + 1 string cheese = 95 calories

Fresh Salads To Go

Yes – you read it right. Convenience stores are now selling pre-packed salads. For a snack, look for salads that are less than 250 calories. Focus on the veggies in the salad and not the extras such as a lot of nuts, crisps, and cheese.

1 salad = 250 calories (calories will vary depending on type of salad bought)

Fresh Vegetables with Dip

Another great option is buying little packs of fresh vegetables like carrots, celery, and cherry tomatoes. They usually come with a dip. Eat less of the dip that is included in the pack to consume less calories.

1 pack of fresh vegetables + 1 pack of light ranch dip = 110 calories

Turkey Sandwich

Following the fresh food trend, you can also buy a turkey sandwich made with just bread and sliced turkey breast.

2 slices bread + 2 ounces lean turkey deli meat = 230 calories

Yogurt with Clementines

Regular yogurt is healthy and delicious. Pair it with a clementine for Vitamin C.

6 ounce plain yogurt + 1 clementine = 140 calories

Many fresh, pre-packaged sandwiches will include mayonnaise and mustard packets on the side. Skip the mayo and just add the mustard for a lower calorie option.

Nonfat Plain Greek Yogurt with Fruit of Choice

Get more fiber by adding your own fruit to nonfat plain Gree
sugar when you put in your own fruit.

5.3 ounce container of nonfat plain Greek yogurt + fruit of ch
(calories may vary depending on what fruit you include)

Nonfat Vanilla Greek Yogurt with Coconut

Pair this protein-packed yogurt with some coconut flake
for extra texture.

5.3 ounce container of nonfat vanilla Greek yogurt +
1 Tablespoon coconut flakes = 160 calories

Light Chicken Noodle Soup

Look for single serve cans or pouches in low-sodium
varieties for a super convenient heat-and-serve snack.

2 cups light chicken noodle soup = 160 calories (calories
will vary depending on brand)

> Many convenient stores offer a microwave for you to use onsite. Buy a soup that is in a microwavable container to enjoy a nourishing, warm snack.

> Soups that are broth-based are lighter and healthier than soups with a cream-base. Look for soups in broths and not in creams. Also try to find reduced-sodium soups.

Chicken Tortilla Soup

One fine example of a delicious, hearty, broth-based soup
that is also healthy.

1 cup chicken tortilla soup = 150 calories (calories will
vary depending on brand)

Black Bean Microwavable Soup

Black beans have protein to help you feel more full.

1 cup black bean soup = 130 calories (calories will vary depending on brand)

Lentil Soup

Lentils are another bean that provides protein, calcium, and potassium. Enjoy this hearty
soup.

1 cup lentil soup = 140 calories (calories will vary depending on brand)

Garden Vegetable Soup

A great way to get your daily dose of veggies is eating this veggie-packed soup.

2 cups garden vegetable soup = 160 calories (calories will vary depending on brand)

Tomato Soup with Cheese Stick

Enjoy a hearty cup of tomato soup with a cheese stick on the side for some protein and satisfaction.

1 cup tomato soup + 1 string cheese = 170 calories (calories will vary depending on brand of soup)

6
CHAPTER

Snacks For Your Sweet Tooth

Every now and then, we want a snack that's on the sweeter side. Especially after dinner, it's also nice to have a mini, portion-controlled sweet snack that's guilt-free.

This section of snacks offers **45 Snacks For Your Sweet Tooth** that are each under 250 calories.

Sweet Potato with Cinnamon and Honey

Roast a small sweet potato that has been pricked with a fork and wrapped in tin foil at 400° degrees for 40 minutes. Remove from oven and add cinnamon and honey for a sweet and simple surprise.

1 small sweet potato (about 1 cup) + 1 Tablespoon honey + 2 teaspoons cinnamon = 220 calories

Peanut Butter, Banana, and Honey Wrap

Spread peanut butter on a whole wheat flour tortilla and top with the banana slices. Drizzle with honey and roll it up. You can warm the wrap on the stove for an extra special treat.

1 whole wheat tortilla + ½ Tablespoon peanut butter + ½ small banana (3 inches, peeled and sliced) + ½ Tablespoon honey + cinnamon for taste = 190 calories

Banana and Chocolate "Quesadilla"

Place the banana slices on top of a small, 6-inch flour tortilla. Cover with 1 Tablespoon of chocolate chips. Fold the tortilla over so you have half a "quesadilla". You can cook on the stove top or place in the microwave to melt the chocolate chips.

1 flour tortilla (6 inches) + 1 small banana (6 inches, peeled and sliced) + 1 Tablespoon chocolate chips = 220 calories

Tortilla with Cinnamon and Agave

Warm a corn tortilla on the stove top or for a few seconds in the microwave. Drizzle agave syrup and sprinkle cinnamon on top for a sweet surprise.

1 small corn tortilla (5 inches) + ½ Tablespoon agave syrup + cinnamon to taste = 115 calories

Cinnamon Toast

Get your favorite slice of bread and toast it. Afterwards, spread it with butter. Sprinkle with cinnamon and sugar. Now, you're in heaven.

1 slice bread + 1 teaspoon butter + 1 teaspoon sugar + 1 teaspoon cinnamon = 145 calories

Baked Apple with Cinnamon Sugar and Peanuts

Mix ½ Tablespoon of brown sugar with a healthy pinch of cinnamon. Core an apple, fill with the sugar mixture, and bake at 375° degrees until apple is fork-tender, about 25 minutes. After the apple is cooked, sprinkle on ½ Tablespoon of crushed peanuts.

1 small apple, cored + ½ Tablespoon brown sugar and cinnamon mixture + ½ Tablespoon crushed peanuts = 108 calories

Grilled Peaches with Cinnamon and Slivered Almonds

Grilled fruit is so delicious. Just light up a grill. Slice a peach in half. Remove the pit. Cook the peach on each side for about 2 minutes. Top with some cinnamon and slivered almonds for a crunchy salty-sweet treat.

1 peach + 1 Tablespoon slivered almonds + cinnamon to taste = 105 calories

Fruit is a naturally sweet treat. Try grilling other fruits like pears, pineapple, mango, or nectarines. Grilling caramelizes some of the sugar in the fruit to provide extra satisfaction for your sweet tooth.

Frozen Grapes and Blueberries with Coconut

This frozen fruit delight is natural, affordable, and very healthy. Put the washed fruit in a container in the freezer. Pull it out when you're ready for a frozen treat. Sprinkle shredded coconut on top for a nice combination.

17 grapes + ¾ cup blueberries + 1 Tablespoon shredded coconut = 138 calories

Cinnamon Applesauce Layered with Ricotta and Honey

Applesauce isn't just for kids anymore – this snack packs fiber, calcium, and satisfies your sweet tooth.

½ cup cinnamon applesauce + ¼ cup low fat ricotta cheese + 1 teaspoon honey = 115 calories

Ricotta, Fruit, and Nut Parfait

Creamy ricotta is thick and rich and a great source of protein and calcium.   A great alternative to an ice cream parfait.

½ cup low fat ricotta + ½ cup sliced strawberries + 6 almonds chopped + 1 teaspoon honey drizzled = 165 calories

Graham Crackers with Ricotta and Strawberries

Spread creamy ricotta on graham crackers and top with sweet fresh strawberries for a delicious snack.

4 graham crackers + ¼ cup low fat ricotta cheese + 1 cup sliced strawberries = 200 calories

Toast with Ricotta, Honey, and Peaches

Spread the ricotta cheese on a slice of whole wheat toast, top with sliced peaches, and drizzle with honey. Yum!

1 slice whole wheat toast + ½ peach, sliced + ¼ cup low fat ricotta cheese + ½ Tablespoon honey = 220 calories

Cheese, Peach, and Dark Chocolate

This surprising combo offers calcium and protein alongside satisfying rich, dark chocolate. Make a nice little plate with these 3 mini treats.

1 mini Babybel® Light cheese round (1 ounce) + 1 small peach + ½ ounce dark chocolate = 200 calories

Cacao Nibs and Dried Pichuberries

For a Peruvian superfood and antioxidant sweet snack: mix together cacao nibs and dried pichuberries. Enjoy a burst of Vitamin C and sweetness. You even get a little protein from the pichuberries.

2 Tablespoons cacao nibs + 2 Tablespoons dried pichuberries = 100 calories

Bananas and Strawberries with Dark Chocolate Chips

Melt the chocolate chips in a small bowl in the microwave for about 20 seconds at a time until melted. Use a spatula to pour the melted chocolate over the sliced bananas and strawberries. Put into the fridge for about 10 minutes for the chocolate to harden.

½ small banana (3 inches, peeled and sliced) + 6 strawberries + ½ ounce of dark chocolate chips = 140 calories

Frozen Banana and Nutella®

This super sweet snack is fantastic and you also get a ton of potassium from the banana. Spread the peeled banana with Nutella®, put it in the freezer for 2 hours and eat it frozen. Delicious!

1 small banana (6 inches, peeled) + 1 Tablespoon Nutella® = 150 calories

Banana, Nutella®, and Peanut Butter

Spread the banana with peanut butter and Nutella to get extra love.

1 small banana (6 inches, peeled) + 1 Tablespoon Nutella® + ½ Tablespoon peanut butter = 230 calories

Date Rolls with Coconut and Whole Almonds

This is an energy booster with natural sweetness. Slice dates open and stuff each date with shredded coconut and 1 almond.

4 whole pitted dates + 1 Tablespoon shredded sweetened coconut + 4 almonds = 230 calories

Dates and Dark Chocolate with Caramel

What more can you ask for in this delicious sweet delicacy? Eat them side by side and savor each wonderful bite.

2 dates + 1 Ghirardelli® Dark Chocolate Caramel Square = 240 calories

Oatmeal Cookie and Canned Peaches

Chewy oatmeal and sweet sliced peaches come together for a delicious treat.

1 oatmeal cookie (1 ounce) + ½ cup canned peaches = 195 calories

Dark Chocolate and Pretzels

Always looking for that salty sweet delight. Mix the two together. You can also melt the chocolate to dip with the pretzels.

22 grams (0.75 ounce) dark chocolate + 1 ounce pretzels = 230 calories

Dark Chocolate and Sliced Banana on Graham Crackers

This twist on the classic s'mores makes for a great sweet treat. Put the dark chocolate on the graham cracker and top with sliced bananas.

½ ounce dark chocolate + ½ small banana (3 inches, peeled and sliced) + 1 graham cracker = 250 calories

Popcorn with Chocolate Shavings

Use air-popped popcorn. Sprinkle a little salt and add chocolate shavings for the salty-sweet combination dessert.

3 cups air-popped popcorn + 1 Tablespoon chocolate shavings + salt to taste = 120 calories

KIND® Dark Chocolate Whole Grain Clusters*

Get ready to enjoy five different super grains coated in dark chocolate and mixed with dark chocolate chunks. Not only will this satisfy any sweet tooth, you'll also get 10 grams of protein with each serving.

½ cup KIND® Dark Chocolate Whole Grain Clusters = 190 calories

These clusters are packed with 25 grams of whole grains. The combination of the whole grains and the protein will provide satiety. KIND® products are made with wholesome ingredients such as oats, millet, brown rice, amaranth, and quinoa.
*Sponsored Product

Vanilla Pudding with Banana

Vanilla and banana are a match made in heaven. This sweet treat is surprisingly low in calories.

1 snack cup of vanilla pudding + ½ small banana (3 inches, peeled and sliced) = 185 calories

You can add any fruit to any flavor of pudding. It's your choice.

Vanilla Pudding with Strawberries

This strawberries and cream combo is healthy and convenient.

1 snack cup of vanilla pudding + ½ cup sliced strawberries = 135 calories

Sugar Free Chocolate Pudding with Fat Free Whipped Topping

This is truly a guilt-free treat for your sweet tooth without sacrificing flavor and/or texture.

1 snack cup no sugar added chocolate pudding + 2 Tablespoons fat free whipped topping = 100 calories

Jell-O® Caramel Crème Mousse Temptations and Sliced Apple

A low calorie version of a classic caramel apple. Use the apple slices to dip into the mousse.

1 snack cup of Jello-O® caramel crème mousse + ½ small apple = 110 calories

Fresh Cherries and Cool Whip

This classic combination is oh-so-summery and fun to eat.

6 ounces of fresh cherries (about 24) + 2 Tablespoons fat free cool whip = 135 calories

Fresh Melon and Cool Whip

Use either cantaloupe or melon and add cool whip for some extra flare.

1 cup cantaloupe (peeled, seeded, and cubed) + 2 Tablespoons fat free cool whip = 75 calories

Add cool whip to any fruit of choice. It will add a touch of decadence to your fiber-filled, delectable fruit dessert.

CranBran VitaMuffin VitaTop® and Raspberries

VitaTop® muffin tops can be found in most stores' freezer sections and pack a punch of fiber, protein, 15 vitamins and minerals, and a healthy serving of whole grains.

1 CranBran VitaMuffin VitaTop® + ½ cup raspberries = 130 calories

Deep Chocolate VitaMuffin VitaTop® and Cool Whip

VitaTop® muffin tops come in so many flavors. Try them all and add fat free cool whip to make a sundae.

1 Deep Chocolate VitaMuffin VitaTop® + 2 Tablespoons fat free cool whip = 120 calories

Blood Orange Sorbet and Arctic Zero® Vanilla Ice Cream

Remember Creamsicle® frozen bars? Try this revamped version of a classic flavor combination for a frozen dessert treat.

½ cup blood orange sorbet + ½ cup Arctic Zero® vanilla ice cream = 160 calories

Skinny Cow® Dreamy Clusters Candy

Crunchy crisps, caramel, and chocolate come together for a sweet treat that doesn't have to break your diet.

1 package (28 grams) Skinny Cow® dreamy clusters candy = 120 calories

Skinny Cow® Heavenly Crisp Candy Bar

Wafers layered with milk chocolate cream are only 110 calories per bar.

I bar (22 grams) Skinny Cow® heavenly crisp candy bar = 110 calories

Yasso® Frozen Greek Yogurt Bar (any flavor)

This frozen Greek yogurt bar gives you a sweet that's packed with protein from the Greek yogurt.

1 bar (65 grams) Yasso® frozen Greek yogurt bar = 70 calories

Blueberry Greek Yogurt Popsicles

Make your own Greek yogurt popsicles. In a blender, blend 1 cup nonfat plain Greek yogurt with 1 cup fresh or frozen blueberries. Pile the mixture into 4 popsicle holders. Place in a freezer for at least 4 hours. Now, you have a frozen, healthy popsicle with fiber and protein. Click <u>HERE</u> to watch the video (or visit <u>SarahKoszyk</u> YouTube channel).

1 popsicle = 55 calories

Dove® Chocolate Covered Almonds

As long as you watch your portion size, these delicious dark chocolate covered nuts are fair game for a quick convenience store snack.

13 pieces of Dove® chocolate covered almonds= 210 calories

Frozen Fruit Juice Bar and Ghirardelli® Dark Chocolate Square

These dessert-like bars are surprisingly all-natural and make a satisfying snack on a hot day.

1 frozen fruit-juice bar + 1 Ghirardelli® dark chocolate square= 240 calories

Nonfat Vanilla Yogurt and Vanilla Wafers

Dip your vanilla wafers in yogurt or crumble them and mix them in for a delicious new take on a parfait.

6 ounces nonfat vanilla yogurt + 4 vanilla wafers = 250 calories

Nonfat Vanilla Yogurt with Grilled Pineapple

Grilling pineapple rings allows the natural sugar from the fruit to get caramelized. Add the pineapple rings to yogurt and you've got a very special sweet treat.

2 grilled pineapple rings + 6 ounces nonfat vanilla yogurt = 180 calories

Nonfat Vanilla Greek Yogurt with Frozen Fruit

Use frozen strawberries, grapes, blueberries, or any frozen fruit to mix with your yogurt. You can buy frozen fruit or make your own by simply putting washed, fresh fruit into a container and freezing for 3-4 hours.

5.3 ounces nonfat vanilla Greek yogurt + 1 cup frozen fruit = 200 calories

Nonfat Plain Greek Yogurt with Honey and Almonds

Greek yogurt gives you more protein per serving than regular yogurt for greater satisfaction. Buy nonfat plain Greek yogurt and add your own honey to sweeten it up. Top with slivered almonds for some salty-crunch.

5.3 ounces of nonfat plain Greek yogurt + 1 Tablespoon honey + 1 Tablespoon slivered almonds = 220 calories

Nonfat Plain Greek Yogurt with Applesauce

Buy nonfat plain Greek yogurt and add applesauce to it for a satisfying treat.

5.3 ounces of nonfat plain Greek yogurt + ½ cup unsweetened applesauce = 175 calories

Peaches N Cream Smoothie

This delicious smoothie is a sweet delight. Just blend everything together and enjoy.

½ peach, sliced + ½ cup nonfat plain yogurt + ½ cup nonfat milk + 1 teaspoon honey + squeeze of lemon juice = 130 calories

7
CHAPTER

Conclusion

How to stay healthy in any snacking situation

Now you have 365 snack ideas for every day of the year and every occasion. Whether you are at home, at school or work, running around town and on the go for the day, stuck on the road with no planning or prepping so your only option is at a convenience store, or even desiring a dessert-like snack for your sweet tooth; you have many options.

Some final takeaways to remember are:

» Always combine at least 2 or more food groups when eating a snack

» Enjoy a protein/carbohydrate snack combination

» Remember to eat every 3 to 4 hours to control your hunger levels, increase your metabolism, and assist with your weight management

» Always remember to have at least one snack a day to stay energized, satiated, and charged.

» If you need to remind yourself to eat that snack, set an alarm in your phone or calendar.

Cheers to happy daily snacking!

Sarah Koszyk, MA, RDN, is an award-winning registered dietitian/ nutritionist specializing in weight management and sports nutrition. Sarah is founder of Family. Food. Fiesta. providing families with delicious and healthy recipes, meal plans, and kid cooking videos in order to optimize one's performance and nutrition. Sarah coaches athletes, adults, and pediatrics towards their health and wellness goals. With a passion for delicious food that nourishes the body, mind, and soul - Sarah emphasizes a holistic approach to learn a sustainable, lifelong, positive relationship with food as fuel for the body. She has been featured on *Bay Sunday CBS San Francisco, Al Despertar Univision 41,* in Runner's World, Today's Dietitian, Fitness Magazine, and more. She has a monthly column in *UltraRunning* Magazine, *NutritionJobs, ExerciseJobs,* and *Swimmer Magazine.* Sarah wrote the book, *25 Anti-Aging Smoothies For Revitalizing, Glowing Skin*. She co-wrote, *Brain Food: 10 Simple Foods That Will Increase Your Focus, Improve Your Memory And Decrease Depression.* Sarah contributed to, *Whole Body Reboot: The Peruvian Superfoods Diet To Detoxify, Energize, And Supercharge Fat Loss*.

Connect with her at www.SarahKoszyk.com and join her fiesta.

Acknowledgements

I would like to thank my Mom and Dad for raising me with an abundance of healthy food options and ideas. Without your guidance and knowledge, I definitely wouldn't be where I am today. Thanks for taking my phone calls at all hours of the night. ☺

I also want to thank the wonderful, talented ladies in my dietetic circle, Yvette Quantz, Liz Weiss, Jessica Setnick, and Katie Ferraro. You each gave me fabulous advice throughout my book writing process. In addition, I want to thank Elizabeth Shaw for always being just a phone call or email away, and constantly sharing her wonderful tips of the trade. You lovely people lift me up and make me a better dietitian.

Last, but not least, I want to give thanks to the love of my life, Tomas (Tommy) King, whose support is so present and prominent. You always have an ear to lend and a perfect stride to chat alongside with. Thank you for being my sounding board and my partner in life. Your photos are amazing and I appreciate all you have taught me regarding the world of lighting. (http://www.studio5designsf.com/).

Made in the USA
San Bernardino, CA
28 June 2017